Interviewing

Principles and Practices

Applications and Exercises

thirteenth edition

Charles J. Stewart

Purdue University

Kendall Hunt
publishing company

Book Team

Chairman and Chief Executive Officer   Mark C. Falb
President and Chief Operating Officer   Chad M. Chandlee
Vice President, Higher Education   David L. Tart
Director of Publishing Partnerships   Paul B. Carty
Editorial Manager   Georgia Botsford
Editor   Melissa M. Tittle
Vice President, Operations   Timothy J. Beitzel
Assistant Vice President, Production Services   Christine E. O'Brien
Senior Production Editor   Mary Melloy
Cover Designer   Jenifer Chapman

www.kendallhunt.com
Send all inquiries to:
4050 Westmark Drive
Dubuque, IA 52004-1840

ISBN 978-0-7575-8437-4

Printed in the United States of America
10 9 8 7 6 5 4 3 2 1

Contents

CONTENTS

About the Author

Charles J. Stewart received his B.S. degree from Indiana State University and his M.A. and Ph.D. degrees from the University of Illinois. He is the former Margaret Church Distinguished Professor of Communication at Purdue University where he taught from 1961 to 2009. He is presently a Professor Emeritus of Communication. He taught undergraduate courses in interviewing and persuasion and graduate courses in such areas as persuasion and social movements, apologetic rhetoric, and extremist rhetoric on the Internet. He teaches workshops in Purdue's Center for Instructional Excellence.

Professor Stewart received five teaching awards from the Department of Communication at Purdue University, the Charles B. Murphy Award for Outstanding Undergraduate Teaching from Purdue University, and the Donald H. Ecroyd Award for Outstanding Teaching in Higher Education from the National Communication Association. He was a Founding Fellow in the Teaching Academy at Purdue University and is listed in Purdue's Book of Great Teachers.

Professor Stewart has served as a consultant to such organizations as the Internal Revenue Service, the American Electric Power Company, the Indiana State Teachers Association, Libby Foods, the United Association of Plumbers and Pipefitters, and the Indiana University School of Dentistry. He is currently a Court Appointed Special Advocate for children (CASA).

Professor Stewart has published articles, chapters, and booklets on interviewing and persuasion. His books include *Interviewing Principles and Practices* (with William B. Cash, Jr.), *Persuasion and Social Movements* (with Craig A. Smith and Robert E. Denton, Jr.), *Teaching Interviewing for Career Preparation*, and *Explorations in Rhetorical Criticism* (with Gerald P. Mohrmann and Donovan J. Ochs).

Preface

This applications and exercises text is designed for courses in the principles and practices of a variety of types of interviews. Such courses, by their nature, require a number of oral and written exercises that build interpersonal communication skills. This text provides students and instructors with a variety of detailed assignments and exercises in the principles of interviewing applicable to most interviews and to specific types of interviewing such as information giving, information getting, journalistic, recruiting, employment, persuasive, performance review, counseling, and health care. Exercises help students learn how to open interviews, develop effective openings and closings, ask questions, answer questions, be active and critical participants, and evaluate interviews. Assignments and critique forms have built-in flexibility so instructors may incorporate them into a variety of courses and units and modify them to meet specific student and course needs.

Instructors may use this text with a number of books and lecture formats, but its maximum use can best be achieved when employed in conjunction with *Interviewing: Principles and Practices* written by Charles J. Stewart and William B. Cash, Jr., and published by McGraw-Hill.

I wish to express my appreciation to the undergraduate students at Purdue University, to present and past colleagues, and particularly to the many graduate students and instructors at Purdue University for their inspiration, suggestions, and criticisms. Special thanks are extended to Suzanne Collins for her many contributions to assignments, exercises, and reporting forms and to Ellen Phelps, Patrice Buzzanell, Mary Alice Baker, and William Seiler.

New for the 13th Edition

This is an extensively revised edition of *Interviewing: Principles and Practices*. It begins with revisions of the **Personal Fact Sheet** and the **Ice Breaker Interview** assignment. All exercises are either new or extensively revised, including:

Types and Uses of Interviews
Approaches to Interviewing
Identification of Questions
Probing Questions
Common Question Pitfalls
Interview Schedules
Question Sequences
Interview Openings and Closings
Information Giving
Survey Interviews
Identification of Survey Question Scales and Strategies
Interviewee Responses to Informational Questions
EEOC Exercise
Recruiter Questions
Responses to Recruiter Questions
Responses to Unlawful Questions
Critical Thinking
Identification of Persuasive Tactics
Tests of Evidence

Two interview assignments are revised, including **Skills Building and Employment**. There is a new **Cover Letter** and a new **Resume for Analysis and Criticism**. A new **Recruiter Workshop for the Employment**

chapter
one

Introduction to Interviewing

Ice Breaker Interview Assignment

The purposes of these brief, ungraded "ice breaker" interviews are: (1) to get you involved immediately in an interview in the classroom setting, (2) to provide you with an opportunity to play the roles of interviewer, interviewee, and observer, and (3) to get an introduction to the complex interview process.

The class will be divided into trios with one student designated A, one designated B, and one designated C. This assignment will go through three rounds of _____ minutes each with students A, B, and C exchanging roles in each round.

Round #1	Round #2	Round #3
A = interviewer	A = observer	A = interviewee
B = interviewee	B = interviewer	B = observer
C = observer	C = interviewee	C = interviewer

Instructions for Interviewers

1. Begin the interview with an appropriate opening when the instructor says **start**.

2. You have a _____ time limit; use all of it.

3. Close the interview with an appropriate closing when the instructor says **stop**.

Instructions for Interviewees

1. Answer all questions thoroughly and honestly.

2. You may tactfully refuse to answer any question you feel is irrelevant or embarrassing.

Instructions for Observers

1. Do not interrupt or distract the interviewer or interviewee.

2. Observe the entire interviewing process, including language, nonverbal communication, and feedback.

3. Do the parties ever switch roles with the interviewer becoming the interviewee or the interviewee becoming the interviewer?

Discussion Questions

1. What language problems did you detect?

2. How would you describe the nonverbal communication between the parties?

3. How well did the parties listen to one another?

4. How did the classroom setting affect the interviews?

5. What types of information did interviewers seek and avoid?

6. Did the parties switch roles at any time?

7. How might preparation have improved these interviews?

Types and Uses of Interviews

The word *interview* creates specific and limited images in our minds. We may visualize a television journalist interviewing a reluctant politician, a recruiter asking questions of a job applicant, or an academic counselor working with a student's problem. The definition in your text suggests that there are many types of interviews, many of which require specific training, abilities, and experiences.

From your own experiences, those portrayed in the media, or ones acquaintances have told you about, **describe in detail a specific situation** for each of the interview types listed below. For instance, have you been in an information giving situation at work, a respondent to a journalist after a sport event, or an applicant for an internship?

Information Giving

Information Getting

Employment

Persuasion

Problems of Interviewee's Behavior

Problem Solving

Health Care

CHAPTER ONE

Approaches to Interviewing Exercise

In every interview, the interviewer must determine which **interviewing approach** is most appropriate: *directive* (in which the interviewer controls the interview), *nondirective* (in which the interviewee controls the interview), or a *combination approach* (in which both parties control the interview from time to time). In each of the situations below, which approach would you select as most appropriate? If you select a combination approach, specify when the interviewer would be in control and when the interviewee would be in control of the interview.

1. A student needs information about a scholarship offered to seniors in his/her field of study.

   Directive

2. A recruiter is conducting screening interviews on campus.

   Combination: Specific questions needed for each E
   Recruiter: when gathering information from candidate   Candidate: asking questions

3. A pre-med student is interviewing several medical school students about what takes place during medical school admissions interviews.

   nondirective

4. An academic counselor is interviewing a student about his/her grade problems in qualifying courses.

   Combination: Nondirective
   Counselor: Asking what is wrong/giving solutions. Student: wanting compromises

5. A market researcher is conducting telephone interviews to assess the effects a recent large recall by an auto manufacturer is having on the image of this auto brand.

   Directive

6. A police officer is interviewing a student who has been assaulted on campus.

   NonDirective

7. A nurse is giving information about the status of patients to a nurse who is coming on duty.

   Directive

8. A supervisor is conducting a quarterly performance review with an employee.

   Directive

9. A human resources staff member is conducting an exit interview with an employee who is leaving for a position with a competitor.

   Combination:
   Combo: HR: Soliciting reasons for why person is leaving
   Emp: Saying why he/she was leaving.

10. A college football recruiter is trying to persuade a star senior at a local high school to accept a scholarship.

   Combo: Directive
   recruiter: Seeing what student wants/telling what the school can give to him

Identification of Questions Exercise

Identify each of the following questions in three ways: (1) open or closed, (2) primary or probing, and (3) neutral or leading. Is it a *special type* of question: bipolar, clearinghouse probe, informational probe, mirror probe, nudging probe, reflective probe, or restatement probe?

1. Are you saying that your plans have changed about leaving the military?

   ~~open, probing, leading~~ ~~informational~~ / Closed - probing - leading, reflective

2. Tell me about your trip to the Super Bowl.

   ~~Closed, Primary, Neutral~~ / Open - primary neutral

3. You're going to the in-service training program, aren't you?

   ~~Closed, mirror probe, neutral~~ / closed - primary - leading

4. What do you think of the budget committee's stupid recommendation to eliminate office telephones?

   Open, primary, leading / op...

5. Do you like horror films?

   ~~Open, primary, neutral~~ / Closed - primary neutral

6. And then?

   ~~Closed, nudging probe, leading~~ / open, probing, neutral - nudging

7. If I understand these types of questions correctly, the reflective probing question literally reflects back on the last answer or two to clarify or verify an interpretation. The mirror question, on the other hand, summarizes a considerable part of the interview to clarify and verify information received. Correct?

   Closed, mirror probe, ~~leading~~ neutral

8. Are you **really** thinking of quitting gymnastics?

   Closed, clearinghouse probe, neutral

9. What have I not asked about the incident that might be important?

   ~~Open, informational probe, neutral leading~~ / open, probing - neutral - clearinghouse

10. Tell me more about the different zebras you saw in Kenya.

   ~~Closed, informational nudging leading~~ / open, probing, neutral - informational

Probing Question Exercise

Provide an appropriate probing question for each interview sequence below. Be sure each question **probes** into the answer and is not a new primary question that delves into a new facet of the interview topic.

1. R = What is your religious affiliation?

   E = I'm a Christian.

   R = Why are you christian / what denomination

2. R = How frequently do you read a printed newspaper?

   E = Occasionally.

   R = How often is occasionally?

3. R = Are you going to the press conference?

   E = I never know.

   R = Why do you never know? / What are your plans right now?

4. R = How was the lecture on diversity?

   E = The usual.

   R = What does that mean?

5. R = How's the new physical therapy working out?

   E = It's a pain; know what I mean?

   R = No, I don't, could you explain?

6. R = Who do you plan to vote for in the mid-term elections?

   E = President Obama.

   R = Why that candidate?

7. R = Are you familiar with the new out-of-state regulations?

   E = Yes.

   R = Will you tell me a few of the major regulations? / How do you know?

8. R = Define team work for me.

   E = (silence)

   R = Do you know what a team is?

9. R = How would you rate the new reality show "Over the Edge?"

   E = Between a two and a three.

   R = Why so low?

10. R = Tell me about school.

    E = The social life on campus is great with lots of parties and chances to get to know people. There are four boys for every two girls. I'm thinking about pledging a sorority next semester.

    R = What would you have to do to pledge?

Common Question Pitfall Exercise

An important way to avoid question pitfalls is to recognize them quickly so you can avoid them during interviews. Each question below commits one or more common question pitfalls: bipolar trap, curious probe, don't ask don't tell, double-barreled inquisition, guessing game, leading push, open-to-closed switch, quiz show, simplicity versus complexity, tell me everything, or yes (no) response.

In this exercise, begin by identifying the pitfall(s) in each question and then rewrite the question to make it a good question. *Avoid committing a new pitfall when rewriting the question.*

1. Tell me about yourself.

   tell me everything – Tell me ab... Something Specific

2. You're coming to the staff meeting, aren't you?

   + leading push – Are you coming to the staff meeting?

3. Tell me about your positions with Mayfield Construction and Lee Remodeling.

   DBI Barreled – Tell me ab your previous employment.

4. I see you're from Springfield. Do you know how Springfield got its name in the 1800s?

   Quiz show –

5. Do you prefer a Toyota or a Honda hybrid?

   Leading push – What kind of car do you prefer.
   OR
   Bipolar trap

6. Would you say you're the smartest player on the team?

   Don't ask, Don't tell – How do you do in Sports?

7. Tell me about your tour in Afghanistan? Were you in danger most of the time?

   Open-to-closed switch → During your tour in Afghan, were you in danger?

8. Did you change academic majors because of the foreign language requirement?

   leading Push
   Guessing game – Why did you change your majors?

9. (Asked in an employment interview) Are your parents college graduates?

   Curious probe
   Don't ask, Don't Tell

10. Do you want to lose a hand in that machine?

    Yes, no

Each type of interview schedule has advantages and disadvantages, depending upon the type of interview being conducted and the interview situation. Review each of the following situations and explain which schedule—nonscheduled, moderately scheduled, highly scheduled, or highly scheduled standardized—you would use and why.

1. You are conducting 15–20 minute interviews for your construction management firm at a college career fair. The interviewees talked with you earlier in the day and gave you copies of their resumes.

   Nonscheduled / moderately

   Moderately scheduled

2. You were off campus at a professional conference when your instructor assigned a field project for your class. You have the assignment requirements but not the due dates for completing each part, so you are meeting with the instructor to obtain these dates.

   Nonscheduled

   Highly Scheduled

3. You are taking a class that focuses on social protest in American history from the Revolution to the present and have been following the Tea Party Movement since its first actions of dumping tea bags in rivers around the country. You have decided to study this protest movement for your final research paper and have made arrangements to interview four people who recently attended the National Tea Party Convention.

   Highly Standardized

   Moderately

4. You are conducting a survey of shoppers at a mall to determine if there is interest in more entertainment options such as a comedy club, an area with a stage for professional and amateur acts, and a dinner theatre.

   Moderately

   Highly Scheduled & Standardized.

5. You are a nurse practitioner who is conducting an in-take interview with a new patient, the purpose of which is to get an overview of the patient's medical history and use of prescription drugs.

Moderately

Question Sequences Exercise

Interviewers have a variety of question sequences from which to choose strategically for all or specific portions of interviews. Describe interview situations when you would use each of the following question sequences.

1. Tunnel sequence

2. Funnel sequence

3. Inverted funnel sequence

4. Hourglass sequence

5. Diamond sequence

Interview Opening Exercise

Review the guidelines for effective interview openings and opening techniques. Write an appropriate opening for each of the following situations that involves the interviewee.

1. You are conducting an in-depth interview with a network sportscaster who was an All-American linebacker in college and was an outstanding linebacker for the New Orleans Saints for nearly ten years. You are particularly interested in how his experiences as a player helped him to attain his position and to become one of the best known sportscasters in the country. The interview was arranged by the interviewee's college coach who is a friend of your family.

    (Hand shake) It's so great to meet you finally, I'm a long time fan & very excited to have this opportunity

    How info will be used, reference.

2. After several years in the real estate field, you started your own agency, Blue Lakes Realty. An acquaintance at your church who has always rented duplexes mentioned recently that she is thinking about purchasing a home in a nicer neighborhood. You have a listing for a single-story home in an upscale neighborhood and have made an appointment to meet the interviewee at a Starbucks to discuss this and other possibilities.

    What are you looking for in a new house?

    Great, thank, state purpose/ summarize issue

3. You are a line supervisor at a Chevrolet assembly plant. When conducting a routine quarterly performance review with Tracinda George, she related a concern about growing animosities among several workers on her shift that have resulted in some pushing and obscene comments between former friends. She claims Jock Demerly seems to be the prime instigator. You have made an appointment near the end of today's shift to interview Jock about the situation. Tracinda has asked that her name not be mentioned.

    The reason we are meeting is because ...

    State purpose, get idea ab work

4. Your neighborhood has always been very safe even though it is not far from the center of a city of 500,000. Recently, however, there have been a number of break-ins during the daytime and three cars have been stolen from driveways. You and five neighbors met a week ago to discuss possible ways to make the neighborhood safe again, and a neighborhood watch idea seemed best. You have agreed to survey residents of the area to determine their interest in forming and being part of a neighborhood watch.

    Hi, my name is ... I live ... . Since the break-ins, I was wondering ...

    Intro... ... Summ...

5. You are an investigative reporter for the *Daily Tribune Star* and have been contacted by a person who wants to blow the whistle on a factory farming operation three miles from town that is allegedly using growth supplements and antibiotics far above the recommended limits of the Meat Producers Association and the Food and Drug Administration. He would not give his name but has arranged to meet you at a local park. You will recognize him by his Irish tweed riding cap and his Irish Setter named Pete. You are to use Pete's name in your greeting.

Hey pete,

Greet, introduce self, Summarize issue, thank

Interview Closing Exercise

Read the situations in the **Interview Opening Exercise** that precedes this exercise and consider how you would recommend that each interview be closed. These and a review of the guidelines for effective interview closings and closing techniques will help you in determining an appropriate closing for each situation.

1. You have been conducting an in-depth interview with a network sportscaster to learn how his experiences as a player helped him to attain his position and to become one of the best known sportscasters in the country. The interview, arranged by the interviewee's college coach who is a family friend, has gone very well but has taken several minutes longer than originally agreed to.

   This has been great, & I am so greatful for meeting you, but I have to leave

   Acknowledge time, apologize, get contact info

2. You have been talking to an acquaintance from church about a real estate listing you have for a single-story home in an upscale neighborhood. Although the interviewee seemed to like the listed home, she has been very noncommittal about this or other listings you mentioned. She does seem interested in moving from her duplex.

   Are there any other questions or concerns you want to discuss?

   Summarize criteria, ask for sale

3. As a line supervisor at a Chevrolet assembly plant, you have been interviewing Jock Demerly accused by another employee of being the prime instigator of animosities among several workers. Jock demanded to know who had accused him of this, but you refused, saying that you had agreed not to identify the source of your information. The interview did not go well, but you have agreed to talk to a sample of workers on Jock's shift to see who is to blame for these alleged animosities.

   This has been educational

   Review next steps, thank for input

4. You have been conducting a survey interview with an 81-year-old resident of your neighborhood about the possibility of starting a neighborhood watch to counteract the rising crime rate in the neighborhood. The interviewee supports the idea in general but has reservations about who would do the watching and the authority they might take on themselves.

   We will bang-out the details soon, we're spreading awareness & gaining members.

   Thank, assure no decision will be made immediately

5. You are an investigative reporter for the *Daily Tribune Star* and have been interviewing a possible whistle blower about alleged misuse of growth supplements and antibiotics at a local factory farming operation. The information from this source is very disturbing and might pose a serious public health issue. The person has refused to provide his name or to name other sources that might support his claims. He was obviously very nervous and abruptly ended the interview after about 15 minutes.

Skills Building Interview Assignment

This assignment is not designed to place you in a "real life" interview setting but to teach you four fundamental interviewing skills that are essential for interviewing:

(1) asking well-designed primary questions

(2) listening carefully to answers to detect clues or problems

(3) asking carefully crafted probing questions to obtain valuable information or to resolve problems with answers

(4) being patient and persistent until you have the information needed

These skills require development and refinement before you can apply them successfully in informational, employment, performance review, persuasive, counseling, or health care interviews. You must learn to listen and to probe to encourage interviewees to continue and to elaborate, obtain all important information in an area, get beyond superficial answers, clarify vague answers, check perceived inaccuracies, and be certain you have obtained and interpreted information accurately. Sharpening these skills will prepare you for later interview assignments that are more "real life," particularly the employment interviews.

This assignment is designed so that you cannot merely ask a series of questions and close the interview once you have completed your list. You are not provided with enough information to develop such a highly scheduled interview. One case consisting of two-to-three pages of facts and testimony from a variety of sources will be used each day of this assignment.

Only the interviewee will know all of the information relevant to a case. Interviewers for each day will know only the information provided in the brief paragraphs listed later in this assignment. At the beginning of each class period, interviewers for the day will leave the room. One interviewer will enter at a time, conduct a complete interview (opening, body, and closing), and take his or her place in the classroom. The class will observe different approaches to getting the same body of facts and testimony, some more successful than others.

You will find this assignment challenging and frustrating because you must rely so heavily on questions created on the spot. Be patient and persistent; do not be too anxious to get on to your next topic or primary question. Be sure to return to your plan of attack or schedule after probing or delving into an important but unplanned area. Do not get side-tracked. You will be surprised how successful you can be in difficult interview situations if you ask good open-ended questions, listen insightfully, ask appropriate probing questions, and remain patient and persistent.

Instructions for Interviewers

1. Each interview will be _____5_____ minutes long.

2. Prepare a moderately scheduled interview: major primary questions and anticipated probing questions. You may bring your written question schedule with you to the interview, but remember that you will not be able to rely solely on a prepared list of questions.

3. Openings should be brief but adequate for the situation. **Involve the interviewee; don't give a monologue.** Assume that you have made an appointment with the interviewee.

4. Your goal is to obtain as much **vital** information as possible in the limited time allowed. You will be graded on how well you conduct the interview, not on how much information you attain.

P's guide 1, Schedules 2, S27 writing implement

5. The interviewee will be honest and helpful but **reticent**. For example, the interviewee will answer bipolar questions with a yes or no or by picking one option given. Open-ended questions will be answered with a sentence or two. The intent is to make you ask carefully crafted primary questions that avoid common question pitfalls, probe insightfully into answers, and be patient and persistent in getting the information you need.

6. Listen carefully to each answer. Do not start thinking about your next primary question until you have all of the information you need from this primary question. Detect important clues.

7. Be patient! Stick with a topic until you have gotten all important and relevant information from the interviewee. If you probe onto a sidetrack for a brief time, do not let this diversion keep you from getting back on the main track. Caution: do not decide too quickly that information you are receiving is unimportant or irrelevant. See where a line of questioning is going before you abandon it.

8. Interviewees are **not involved** in the case. They are merely sources of facts and testimony you need, so do not waste time trying to discover how and why an interviewee has the information.

9. Your interview will be worth _____ points.

Instructions for Interviewees

1. Know your case thoroughly so you can give information accurately without hesitation.

2. Listen carefully to each question so you can respond appropriately. **Do not volunteer information**; make the interviewer ask for it.

3. Answer bipolar and yes (no) questions exactly as they are asked, with a yes or no or few words. Answer only one part of double-barreled questions. Answer the last question of open-to-closed switch questions. Give a sentence or two to open questions. Make the interviewer aware of question pitfalls.

4. Drop an occasional clue to see if the interviewer will pick it up and probe effectively.

5. Your interview will be worth _____ points.

The following cases will be used for this assignment: numbers _____

Case #1—John T. Johnson was stopped and arrested in a Chicago park. There has been a hearing, and Johnson has brought charges against the arresting officers. You are interested in this case because similar incidents have happened in your neighborhood. The interviewee attended the hearing and knows the facts and testimony given thus far. You will relate your findings to the Lincoln Neighborhood Association.

Case #2—Jane Manly is suing Virginia Packman for negligence that caused a painful injury. A preliminary court hearing has been held, and the case is now scheduled for a jury trial. You are a pre-law student interested in negligence cases and have arranged an interview with a person who knows the facts and testimony.

Case #3—Arthur Nichols is suing William Parry for damages, costs, and lost income. You are a sociology student interested in neighborhood conflicts and have contacted a person who has collected facts and testimony on the Nichols-Parry case.

Case #4—Giulo Giordano has been accused of cheating at Brier University. A hearing has been held but no decision has been made. You are a student interested in student rights and have arranged an interview with a person who attended the hearing and knows the facts of the case and testimony given.

Case #5—Several years ago a natural disaster struck a Boy Scout camp near Elizabeth, Tennessee. Local residents have recently written to the Baker Hero Fund Commission urging that Rex Ingram be awarded its silver medal for his actions during the disaster. The Baker Commission has sent you to Elizabeth to interview a person who has the facts and statements from residents.

Case #6—Marian Williams has had her teaching contract terminated in mid-year by the Oak Park school board. You are a student interested in labor and management disputes and have driven to Oak Park to interview a person who knows the facts and testimony available at this time.

Case #7—William McCollum, a farmer in Smithfield, North Dakota, has died and left an estate. His children are contesting the will. A friend of yours is in a similar situation and you have agreed to interview a person who knows the family background and heard witnesses at a recent hearing.

Case #8—Jessie Gustavson and her aunt were stopped as they were leaving a restaurant, and Jessie is suing the restaurant. An initial hearing has been held. As a student in restaurant and hotel management who plans to manage a restaurant, you have decided to write a research paper on this case. You have set up an interview with a person who can report the facts and testimony pertaining to this situation.

Case #9—Several years ago Mathew Harvey was shot and killed outside of his home in Westfield, Alabama. A trial was held but no convictions were ever made. You are a history student who would like to write a student honors paper on this case and trial. You have located a former resident of Westfield who attended all sessions of the trial and knows a great deal about the case.

Case #10—After a wild chase through New York City, police managed to stop a taxi reported to be carrying bandits who held up a company. Patrolman Dempsey shot and killed the driver as he emerged from the taxi. Dempsey is now being accused of manslaughter, and a hearing has been held. You are an intern with the Elizabeth, New Jersey *Courier & Times* and have arranged an interview with a person who attended the hearing and knows the facts and testimony given.

Opening
Introduce yourself
State name & company
Reveal the purpose

Skills Building Interview Critique: Form A

Interviewer _____   Critic _____

Opening . . . . 1 2 3 4 5 × _____ = _____

Conducting the interview

       Primary questions . . . . 1 2 3 4 5 × _____ = _____

       Avoidance of question pitfalls . . . . 1 2 3 4 5 × _____ = _____

       Probing questions . . . . 1 2 3 4 5 × _____ = _____

       Patience and persistence . . . . 1 2 3 4 5 × _____ = _____

       Focus on critical areas . . . . 1 2 3 4 5 × _____ = _____

Overall structure . . . . 1 2 3 4 5 × _____ = _____

Closing . . . . 1 2 3 4 5 × _____ = _____

Communication skills . . . . 1 2 3 4 5 × _____ = _____

Total Points _____

Comments:

Grading Scale:

   1 poor
   2 below average
   3 average
   4 above average
   5 excellent

Skills Building Interview Critique: Form A

Interviewer _____ Critic _____

Opening . . . . 1 2 3 4 5 × _____ = _____

Conducting the interview

    Primary questions . . . . 1 2 3 4 5 × _____ = _____

    Avoidance of question pitfalls . . . . 1 2 3 4 5 × _____ = _____

    Probing questions . . . . 1 2 3 4 5 × _____ = _____

    Patience and persistence . . . . 1 2 3 4 5 × _____ = _____

    Focus on critical areas . . . . 1 2 3 4 5 × _____ = _____

Overall structure . . . . 1 2 3 4 5 × _____ = _____

Closing . . . . 1 2 3 4 5 × _____ = _____

Communication skills . . . . 1 2 3 4 5 × _____ = _____

Total Points _____

Comments:

Grading Scale:
    1 poor
    2 below average
    3 average
    4 above average
    5 excellent

Skills Building Interview Critique: Form B

Interviewer _____ Critic _____

Opening: greeting, rapport building, orientation, appropriate techniques, involvement of the interviewee

Points _____

Overall structure: moderately scheduled, flexible, adaptive

Points _____

Use of questions: primary questions, probing questions, avoidance of common question pitfalls

Points _____

Conducting the interview: stress on important data, patience and persistence, maintains rapport, note taking, use of time

Points _____

Communication skills: verbal, nonverbal, listening

Points _____

Closing: appropriate techniques, future appointment if necessary, ends on a positive note, involvement of the interviewee

Points _____

Total Points _____

Skills Building Interview Critique: Form B

Interviewer _____ Critic _____

Opening: greeting, rapport building, orientation, appropriate techniques, involvement of the interviewee

Points _____

Overall structure: moderately scheduled, flexible, adaptive

Points _____

Use of questions: primary questions, probing questions, avoidance of common question pitfalls

Points _____

Conducting the interview: stress on important data, patience and persistence, maintains rapport, note taking, use of time

Points _____

Communication skills: verbal, nonverbal, listening

Points _____

Closing: appropriate techniques, future appointment if necessary, ends on a positive note, involvement of the interviewee

Points _____

Total Points _____

Skills Building Interview Critique: Form B

Interviewer _____ Critic _____

Opening: greeting, rapport building, orientation, appropriate techniques, involvement of the interviewee

Points _____

Overall structure: moderately scheduled, flexible, adaptive

Points _____

Use of questions: primary questions, probing questions, avoidance of common question pitfalls

Points _____

Conducting the interview: stress on important data, patience and persistence, maintains rapport, note taking, use of time

Points _____

Communication skills: verbal, nonverbal, listening

Points _____

Closing: appropriate techniques, future appointment if necessary, ends on a positive note, involvement of the interviewee

Points _____

Total Points _____

Informational Interviewing

Information Giving Exercise

Every day we are involved in giving information to another party, but few communication activities seem as simple as giving pieces of information or instructions. This apparent simplicity is quite deceiving, however, because we neither give nor receive information effectively. Even highly motivated people such as medical patients forget or confuse information within minutes or a few hours.

This exercise is designed to make you aware of the problems in transmitting and receiving information and ways to improve both activities through effective sending and retaining information. Your instructor will use three paragraphs such as the following:

> *We are going to have the reception at the city park just south of town at 8:30. Take a hard left at the Court House and go several blocks past the old fire station. Turn right onto North Wilmington for a short time until you see a large oak tree near the corner of South. Turn left into a parking lot of an insurance agency. The park is to the left and the pedestrian entrance will take you to the community building.*

At the start of this exercise, four to six students will leave the room. Your instructor will read the message to the first student who reenters the room, and this student will pass the message from memory to the next student who reenters. This process continues until the last student transmits the message to the class. Students not sent to the hall receive copies of the message so they can observe what happens (omissions, changes, distortions, additions) as it is passed orally and from memory from student to student.

A second message is selected and four to six students are sent out of the room. The procedure is the same except that each student may ask three simple questions about the content of the message *after* hearing it. How do these questions aid in retention of the original message?

A third paragraph is selected and four to six students are sent out of the room. The procedure is the same except that each party *repeats* the message immediately after the first transmission. How does repetition aid in retention of the original message?

Causes of Information Loss and Distortion

Which of the following seemed to cause problems in accurate transmission and retention of the messages passed from student to student?

1. The physical setting (noise, seating, furniture, gadgets, lack of privacy, classroom setting)

2. Interviewer restrictions (memory, ability to listen, ability to comprehend, nervousness, health)

3. Perceived similarities and differences between interviewer and interviewee (male to female, age differences, instructor to student, senior to freshman, superior to subordinate)

4. Relationship of interviewer and interviewee (degree of trust, degree of affection/liking, desire to be included or involved, degree of control)

5. Transmission techniques (how information was transmitted, when and how questions were asked, how repetitions were made, language, loudness or softness of voice, pronunciation of and emphasis on words)

6. Information overload (amount, details, and complexity)

7. Attitudes toward the subject matter (interest, hostility, perceived importance)

8. Situational barriers (time of day or week, past or future events, in front of others)

9. Natural tendencies (to make sense of information, fill in gaps, add missing pieces)

Ways to Improve Accuracy of Transmission and Retention of Information

Be aware that each of us transmits and retains information differently. Some of us recall names, events, dates, and directions by associating them with people, places, or things we remember easily. For instance, we may give directions or retain them best by identifying things along the way: a large oak tree, a big red house, a grade school, a bridge, stoplight, or a McDonald's. Others may give directions or retain them by providing street names, highway numbers, and compass points. Know yourself and know your audience.

The following suggestions may enhance the way you transmit and retain information.

1. Improve content presentation of information by:

    a. Using visual aids and handouts

    b. Presenting information systematically

    c. Employing previews and reviews of information

    d. Defining key terms and concepts

    e. Transmitting only relevant and important information

    f. Repeating important words and data strategically and throughout the interview

2. Improve the nonverbal presentation of the message by:

    a. Using models, objects, maps, pictures, and drawings

    b. Watching and listening for feedback

    c. Using vocal emphasis (oral highlighting), and pauses (oral punctuation) that call attention to important words, names, numbers, and qualifiers

3. Engage the other party in information giving interviews by:

    a. Answering questions *during* the interview

    b. Promoting active listening

    c. Asking the interviewee to repeat points, steps, names, directions, facts, and instructions

    d. Encouraging note taking and recording

4. Reduce the number of persons through whom the message passes.

5. Other ways to enhance the transmissions and retention of information:

    a.

    b.

    c.

    d.

Survey Interview Exercise

Survey interviews are carefully planned and executed because they must produce accurate, reliable data from multiple interviewees that will enable the survey creator to generalize to large populations of people, draw sound conclusions, make predictions, and perhaps to plan for the future. This exercise enables you to apply the theory, research, and principles presented in your textbook to a specific survey situation. It focuses on the decisions you must make before you develop an interview guide and a highly standardized schedule of questions.

Setting

Many years ago your university, like many throughout the country, developed a school calendar that placed the start of the Fall semester in the third week of August and the end of the fall semester just before the Christmas break. The Spring semester started in early January and ended in the first week of May.

There is now a move by some faculty, administrators, and students at your university and some members of the state legislature to move the calendar back to the time when fall classes started after Labor Day and ended in mid-to-late January. The spring semester started in late January and ended in the first or second week of June.

You have been asked by the University Senate (consisting of faculty, administration, and staff) and the Student Government to conduct a survey of student attitudes about possible changes in the school calendar that would start the school year after Labor Day and end it in early June. You must have your report ready within six weeks with a budget of $2000.00 to cover expenses and small stipends for student interviewers.

You have never conducted a survey, so you have made arrangements to attend a course in interviewing principles and practices to obtain advice and assistance in creating and conducting this survey. The class members are your *experts* and will be ready to answer questions such as the following:

1. What *research* should I conduct *before* considering a guide and schedule of questions?

2. Should I conduct a *cross-sectional* or a *longitudinal* study?

3. What is the *population* or *target group* for this survey?

4. How *many* members of this population or target group must I interview?

5. What *margin of error* should I strive for in this survey?

6. Since I cannot interview *all members* of my population or target audience, which *sampling method* should I employ?

7. Where should interviewers conduct these survey interviews?

8. Would it be okay to conduct *some* of the interviews over the *telephone*?

9. Would it be okay to conduct *some* of the interviews through the *Internet*?

10. What type of *interview schedule* should I develop?

Identification of Survey Question Scales and Strategies

This is a survey of parents concerning their children's use of the Internet. Identify the following survey question *scales* (evaluative interval, frequency interval, nominal, ordinal, Bogardus Social Distance) and *strategies* (filter, repeat, leaning, shuffle, chain).

1. Do you control your children's use of the Internet at home?

   _____ Yes

   _____ No

2. How many hours a day do your children use the Internet at home?

   _____ 4 or more hours

   _____ 3 hours

   _____ 2 hours

   _____ 1 hour

   _____ less than one hour

3. Do you strongly agree, agree, disagree, or strongly disagree with the statement that use of the Internet is essential to your children's education?

   _____ strongly agree

   _____ agree

   _____ neither agree nor disagree

   _____ disagree

   _____ strongly disagree

4. Please rank the following possible educational benefits of the Internet in order of importance for your children. (Rotate order of the benefits from interview to interview.)

   _____ reservoir of information

   _____ aid to research

   _____ assistance with homework

   _____ teacher aid

   _____ extension of knowledge learned in the classroom

   _____ motivator to explore on their own

5a. Do you allow your children to use the Internet without restrictions? (If the answer is "No," ask question 5b.)

   _____ Yes

   _____ No

5b. What restrictions do you apply?

_____

_____

6a. Would you prefer to have your children in a traditional classroom or to take courses on-line? (Ask q. 6b if not sure/undecided.)

_____ traditional classroom

_____ on-line

_____ not sure/undecided

6b. Which do you lean to at this time?

_____ traditional classroom

_____ on-line

_____ not sure/undecided

7. How would you rate the quality of the Internet resources your children have used in preparing homework, reports, and papers for the following courses on a scale of 5 being excellent, 4 good, 3 average, 2 below average, and 1 poor?

	Excellent	Good	Average	Below Average	Poor
Science	5	4	3	2	1
Mathematics	5	4	3	2	1
English	5	4	3	2	1
History	5	4	3	2	1
Art	5	4	3	2	1

8. On-line courses are becoming common throughout the United States.

   a. Do you think there is a need for more on-line courses in this country?

   _____ Yes _____ No

   b. Do you think there is a need for more on-line courses in your state?

   _____ Yes _____ No

   c. Do you think there is a need for more on-line courses in your county?

   _____ Yes _____ No

   d. Do you think there is a need for more on-line courses in your city?

   _____ Yes _____ No

   e. Do you think there is a need for more on-line courses in your children's schools?

   _____ Yes _____ No

9. Which of these possible features concern you the most when your children are using the Internet without supervision?

    a. _____ Personal revelations on Facebook

    b. _____ Pornography

    c. _____ Opinions counter to your family's values

    d. _____ Violent games

    e. _____ Development of harmful relationships with unknown adults

10. I am going to read you several income levels. Stop me when I have exceeded the limit of your annual family income.

    _____ $20,000 to $29,000

    _____ $30,000 to $39,000

    _____ $40,000 to $49,000

    _____ $50,000 to $59,000

    _____ $60,000 to $70,000

    _____ Above $70,000

11. Which is the highest grade level you attained in school?

    _____ 8–11 years

    _____ High school graduate

    _____ Some college

    _____ College graduate

    _____ Master's degree

    _____ Doctorate

Interviewee Responses to Informational Questions

As an interviewee, you must learn how to reply to questions strategically and effectively. Review the principles and strategies for answering questions in informational interviews and then: (1) identify the problem or problems with each question below, and (2) provide an answer you might give *to your advantage*.

You are a senior guard on your college's women's basketball team that seems destined to be a Final Four team in this year's NCAA national tournament. A reporter for the local paper is interviewing you just prior to your final regular season, home contest.

1. How do you feel about your chances of making the Final Four this year? Do you think you will make it?

2. What do you know about the other Top 20 teams this year?

3. Do you consider yourself to be the top player on your team?

4. What is your basketball philosophy?

5. There has been a lot of controversy this year about team mascots. Don't you think that's blown out of proportion?

6. How would you feel if you got hurt in this final regular season game?

7. Drinking has gotten many athletes in trouble this year. Which of these actions do you think schools should take when an athlete is arrested for underage drinking or being drunk: suspension for three games after the first incident, suspension for the season after the second incident, dismissal from the team after a third incident, tight curfew hours during the season, off limits for all establishments that serve alcohol after 10:00 p.m., apply the same standards applied to all students?

8. Tell me about yourself.

9. What is your personal, non-player relationship with your coach?

10. What does it take to make you play your best basketball?

Informational Interview Assignment

This assignment provides you with a realistic experience in conducting a complete, moderately scheduled, informational interview that builds upon the basic skills studied in the first two units of this course and practice in the skills building interview assignment. Your specific goal in this assignment is to learn everything you can about the interviewee's *career* preparation, work experiences, employment interviewing experiences, plans, and short-range and long-range goals. It is not a biographical interview.

This assignment helps you prepare for the next unit on employment interviewing and thinking of your own career preparation. You are involved in interviews such as these when you discuss careers with fellow students, professors, academic counselors, recruiters at job fairs, and family members. You use these interviewing skills when gathering information to introduce a guest or speaker, to prepare a paper or report for a class, and to learn about an organization and position before an employment interview. Journalists, recruiters, and supervisors conducting performance reviews devote major portions of interviews to discussions of career options, plans, and preparation.

This interview assignment continues to emphasize the basic skills practiced in the skills building assignment: structure, use of primary and probing questions, listening, and verbal and nonverbal communication skills. Develop an interview guide that covers the major topics and subtopics you think are relevant for a "career interview." Then turn this interview guide into a moderately scheduled interview with possible probing questions placed under primary questions.

Remember a central point emphasized in your textbook and this course: you must be prepared to adapt your schedule and questions as you go along because you can never know for sure how an interviewee will answer or react. Your interviewee may have only vague career plans and goals, be struggling to choose among several career options, be in the selected career now, or have been in several careers already and be in the process of changing. Your interviewee will be assigned to you the day of your interview, so there will be no opportunity to get to know the person in advance.

Instructions for Interviewers

1. Prepare an interview guide of relevant and interesting major topics and subtopics that focus on career preparation, work experiences, interview experiences, plans, and goals. The chapters in your textbook on employment interviewing can help you select topics.

2. Prepare a moderately scheduled interview from your guide that contains primary questions and possible probing questions. Give a copy of this schedule to your instructor no later than _____.

3. You may bring your written schedule of questions to the interview, but you must be *flexible* and *adaptable*. Merely reading a list of prepared questions shows you are not listening carefully for clues and answers that are incomplete, superficial, vague, suggestible, irrelevant, or inaccurate. Effective probing into answers using both prepared and unprepared probing questions is a major thrust of this assignment. And heavy reliance upon your schedule may stifle effective communication between you and your interviewee.

4. Openings and closings should be brief but adequate.

5. Take working notes that would enable you to write a detailed report of your findings at a later date.

6. The interviews will be _____ minutes long.

7. Each interview will be worth _____ points.

Instructions for Interviewees

1. Come to the class period during which you will serve as an interviewee prepared to discuss your career preparation, work experiences, interview experiences, plans, and goals.

2. Answer questions according to the question type asked. For example, give a yes or a no or select one option when the interviewer asks a bipolar question. Answer open-ended questions with two or three sentences. Answer one part of a double-barreled question. Answer the last question in an open-to-closed switch question. Part of your task is to force your interviewer to practice listening and probing skills and to recognize common question pitfalls.

3. Answer questions honestly, but you may tactfully refuse to answer any question you feel is irrelevant to the assignment or is none of the interviewer's business.

4. Listen carefully to each question so you can answer appropriately and insightfully.

5. Do not purposely distract or mislead your interviewer.

6. Each interview will be worth _____ points.

Informational Interview Critique: Interviewer Form A

Interviewer _____ Critic _____

Opening . . . . 1 2 3 4 5 ✕ _____ = _____

Conducting the interview

      Primary questions . . . . 1 2 3 4 5 ✕ _____ = _____

      Avoidance of question pitfalls . . . . 1 2 3 4 5 ✕ _____ = _____

      Probing questions . . . . 1 2 3 4 5 ✕ _____ = _____

      Patience and persistence . . . . 1 2 3 4 5 ✕ _____ = _____

      Focus on critical areas . . . . 1 2 3 4 5 ✕ _____ = _____

Overall structure . . . . 1 2 3 4 5 ✕ _____ = _____

Closing . . . . 1 2 3 4 5 ✕ _____ = _____

Communication skills . . . . 1 2 3 4 5 ✕ _____ = _____

Total Points _____

Comments:

Grading Scale:
    1 poor
    2 below average
    3 average
    4 above average

Informational Interview Critique: Interviewer Form A

Interviewer _____ Critic _____

Opening . . . . 1 2 3 4 5 × _____ = _____

Conducting the interview

      Primary questions . . . . 1 2 3 4 5 × _____ = _____

      Avoidance of question pitfalls . . . . 1 2 3 4 5 × _____ = _____

      Probing questions . . . . 1 2 3 4 5 × _____ = _____

      Patience and persistence . . . . 1 2 3 4 5 × _____ = _____

      Focus on critical areas . . . . 1 2 3 4 5 × _____ = _____

Overall structure . . . . 1 2 3 4 5 × _____ = _____

Closing . . . . 1 2 3 4 5 × _____ = _____

Communication skills . . . . 1 2 3 4 5 × _____ = _____

                                                Total Points _____

Comments:

Grading Scale:
    1 poor
    2 below average
    3 average
    4 above average
    5 excellent

Informational Interview Critique: Interviewer Form B

Interviewer _____ Critic _____

Opening: greeting, rapport building, orientation, appropriate techniques, involves the interviewee

Points _____

Structure: moderately scheduled, flexible, adaptive

Points _____

Use of questions: primary questions, probing questions, avoidance of common question pitfalls

Points _____

Conducting the interview: focus on relevant topics, patience and persistence, maintains rapport, note taking, use of time allowed

Points _____

Communication skills: verbal, nonverbal, listening

Points _____

Closing: appropriate techniques, ends on a positive note, involves the interviewee

Points _____

Total Points _____

Informational Interview Critique: Interviewer Form B

Interviewer _____ Critic _____

Opening: greeting, rapport building, orientation, appropriate techniques, involves the interviewee

Points _____

Structure: moderately scheduled, flexible, adaptive

Points _____

Use of questions: primary questions, probing questions, avoidance of common question pitfalls

Points _____

Conducting the interview: focus on relevant topics, patience and persistence, maintains rapport, note taking, use of time allowed

Points _____

Communication skills: verbal, nonverbal, listening

Points _____

Closing: appropriate techniques, ends on a positive note, involves the interviewee

Points _____

Total Points _____

Informational Interview Critique: Interviewer Form B

Interviewer _____ Critic _____

Opening: greeting, rapport building, orientation, appropriate techniques, involves the interviewee

Points _____

Structure: moderately scheduled, flexible, adaptive

Points _____

Use of questions: primary questions, probing questions, avoidance of common question pitfalls

Points _____

Conducting the interview: focus on relevant topics, patience and persistence, maintains rapport, note taking, use of time allowed

Points _____

Communication skills: verbal, nonverbal, listening

Points _____

Closing: appropriate techniques, ends on a positive note, involves the interviewee

Points _____

Total Points _____

Informational Interview Critique: Interviewee Form A

Interviewee _____ Critic _____

Participation in the opening . . . . 1 2 3 4 5 × _____ = _____

Interview preparation . . . . 1 2 3 4 5 × _____ = _____

Answering questions . . . . 1 2 3 4 5 × _____ = _____

Communication skills . . . . 1 2 3 4 5 × _____ = _____

Participation in closing . . . . 1 2 3 4 5 × _____ = _____

Total Points _____

Comments:

Grading Scale:

    1 poor
    2 below average
    3 average
    4 above average
    5 excellent

Informational Interview Critique: Interviewee Form A

Interviewee _____ Critic _____

Participation in the opening . . . . 1 2 3 4 5 × _____ = _____

Interview preparation . . . . 1 2 3 4 5 × _____ = _____

Answering questions . . . . 1 2 3 4 5 × _____ = _____

Communication skills . . . . 1 2 3 4 5 × _____ = _____

Participation in closing . . . . 1 2 3 4 5 × _____ = _____

Total Points _____

Comments:

Grading Scale:

1 poor
2 below average
3 average
4 above average
5 excellent

Informational Interview Critique: Interviewee Form B

Interviewee _____ Critic _____

_____

Participation in the opening

Points _____

Interview preparation: familiarity with the topic, anticipation of questions

Points _____

Answering questions: phrasing, to the point, appropriate length, accurate information, to personal advantage, answer strategies

Points _____

Communication skills: verbal, nonverbal, listening

Points _____

Participation in the closing

Points _____

Total Points _____

Informational Interview Critique: Interviewee Form B

Interviewee _____ Critic _____

_____

Participation in the opening

Points _____

Interview preparation: familiarity with the topic, anticipation of questions

Points _____

Answering questions: phrasing, to the point, appropriate length, accurate information, to personal advantage, answer strategies

Points _____

Communication skills: verbal, nonverbal, listening

Points _____

Participation in the closing

Points _____

Total Points _____

Informational Interview Critique: Interviewee Form B

Interviewee _____ Critic _____

_____

Participation in the opening

Points _____

Interview preparation: familiarity with the topic, anticipation of questions

Points _____

Answering questions: phrasing, to the point, appropriate length, accurate information, to personal advantage, answer strategies

Points _____

Communication skills: verbal, nonverbal, listening

Points _____

Participation in the closing

Points _____

Total Points _____

Employment Interviewing

Employment Interviewing Assignment

You are now ready to apply the interviewing principles learned in the first two units of this course: interpersonal communication, listening, questioning, structuring, information getting, and information giving. All of these skills are critical when you are a recruiter or applicant in an employment selection interview. Each interview is a blend of informing, information gathering, and persuading because both parties must give and get information while convincing the other that he or she is the ideal applicant for this position or that this position with this organization at this time is ideal for this applicant. The goal is two perfect fits.

This assignment provides you with two highly realistic employment interviewing experiences: one as a recruiter and one as an applicant. It is important to see the selection process from both sides of the table because you will play both roles in your professional and social lives. Though you are undoubtedly most interested in the applicant role at this stage in your life as you seek internships and positions, you will play the role of recruiter far more often in the future than the role of applicant.

You are likely to be an applicant only a few times in your life, but you are likely to be involved continually in the recruiting process with organizations that employ you, regardless of your job description. You are also likely to be involved in "social" hiring such as selecting clergy for your church, superintendents for your children's school system, directors for local music groups, and candidates for your political party. As a bonus, understanding what the recruiter does and why will make you a more effective applicant.

Student recruiters in this assignment will assume the role of screening interviewers for organizations. Student applicants will assume the role of college seniors seeking entry level positions. No other role playing is necessary for this assignment.

Instructions for Applicants

Make
2 copies

1. Fill out a **Position Description Form** for a real position with a real organization you would like to attain upon graduation. Give a copy of this form to your assigned recruiter and your instructor by _____Oct 19th_____. Details are important because your assigned recruiter will work for this organization seeking to fill the position you describe and must become familiar with both position and organization.

2. Complete a resume and write an application letter for the position you have selected. Present copies of these to your recruiter and instructor no later than _____Oct. 21_____. Make all information real except for projecting yourself to the last semester of your senior year if you are not yet a senior.

3. Develop a moderate schedule of questions that you will ask.

4. Come to the interview dressed appropriately for a formal, professional meeting.

5. Applicants may attain a possible _____ points for this assignment (including position description form, resume, letter of application, and interview).

Instructions for Recruiters

1. Complete in detail the **Recruiter Worksheet for the Employment Interview** and give it to your instructor no later than _____.

2. Develop a moderate schedule of questions based on the applicant profile for this position and the applicant's resume and letter of application. Be sure to include challenging questions that reveal the applicant's ability to perform the demands of the position at a high level, including *behavior-based questions, critical incident questions,* and *hypothetical questions*).

3. Prepare information to give the applicant on the position and organization.

4. Follow the interview guide presented in this text and your textbook.

5. The interview will be _____ minutes long plus a closing. An approximate time distribution might be:

   ☐ One and a half minutes for the opening that *involves the applicant*

   ☐ Eight to nine minutes for recruiter questions

   ☐ Two to three minutes for information giving

   ☐ Three minutes of applicant questions

   ☐ One minute for the closing that *involves the applicant.*

6. Recruiters are responsible for appropriate use and division of time. Bring a watch with you and use it to keep close track of time.

Note: Use all allotted time for this assignment. If an applicant uses only a minute or two to ask questions, resume asking your questions.

7. Come to the interview dressed appropriately for a formal, professional meeting.

8. Recruiters may attain a possible _____ points for this assignment (including the **Recruiter Worksheet** and the interview).

Employment Interview Critique: Recruiter Form A

Recruiter _____ Critic _____

Opening . . . . 1 2 3 4 5 × _____ = _____

Body of the interview

       Primary questions . . . . 1 2 3 4 5 × _____ = _____

       Avoids question pitfalls . . . . 1 2 3 4 5 × _____ = _____

       Probing questions . . . . 1 2 3 4 5 × _____ = _____

       Covers key profile areas . . . . 1 2 3 4 5 × _____ = _____

       Provides information . . . . 1 2 3 4 5 × _____ = _____

       Answers applicant's questions . . . . 1 2 3 4 5 × _____ = _____

Closing . . . . 1 2 3 4 5 × _____ = _____

Use and division of time . . . . 1 2 3 4 5 × _____ = _____

Appearance and dress . . . . 1 2 3 4 5 × _____ = _____

Communication skills . . . . 1 2 3 4 5 × _____ = _____

Total Points _____

Comments:

Grading Scale:

    1 poor

    2 below average

    3 average

    4 above average

Employment Interview Critique: Recruiter Form A

Recruiter _____ Critic _____

Opening . . . . 1 2 3 4 5 × _____ = _____

Body of the interview

     Primary questions . . . . 1 2 3 4 5 × _____ = _____

     Avoids question pitfalls . . . . 1 2 3 4 5 × _____ = _____

     Probing questions . . . . 1 2 3 4 5 × _____ = _____

     Covers key profile areas . . . . 1 2 3 4 5 × _____ = _____

     Provides information . . . . 1 2 3 4 5 × _____ = _____

     Answers applicant's questions . . . . 1 2 3 4 5 × _____ = _____

Closing . . . . 1 2 3 4 5 × _____ = _____

Use and division of time . . . . 1 2 3 4 5 × _____ = _____

Appearance and dress . . . . 1 2 3 4 5 × _____ = _____

Communication skills . . . . 1 2 3 4 5 × _____ = _____

Total Points _____

Comments:

Grading Scale:
   1 poor
   2 below average
   3 average
   4 above average

Employment Interview Critique: Recruiter Form B

Recruiter _____ Critic _____

Opening: greeting, rapport, orientation, involves the applicant

Points _____

Questions: primary questions, avoids pitfalls, probing questions

Points _____

Conducting the interview: covers key profile areas, provides information, answers questions

Points _____

Closing

Points _____

Appropriate use and division of time

Points _____

Appearance and dress

Points _____

Communication skills: verbal, nonverbal, listening

Points _____

Total Points _____

Employment Interview Critique: Recruiter Form B

Recruiter _____ Critic _____

_____

Opening: greeting, rapport, orientation, involves the applicant

Points _____

Questions: primary questions, avoids pitfalls, probing questions

Points _____

Conducting the interview: covers key profile areas, provides information, answers questions

Points _____

Closing

Points _____

Appropriate use and division of time

Points _____

Appearance and dress

Points _____

Communication skills: verbal, nonverbal, listening

Points _____

Total Points _____

Employment Interview Critique: Recruiter Form B

Recruiter _____ Critic _____

Opening: greeting, rapport, orientation, involves the applicant

Points _____

Questions: primary questions, avoids pitfalls, probing questions

Points _____

Conducting the interview: covers key profile areas, provides information, answers questions

Points _____

Closing

Points _____

Appropriate use and division of time

Points _____

Appearance and dress

Points _____

Communication skills: verbal, nonverbal, listening

Points _____

Total Points _____

Employment Interview Critique: Applicant Form A

Applicant _____ Critic _____

Active part in opening .... 1 2 3 4 5 × _____ = _____

Body

        Answers questions .... 1 2 3 4 5 × _____ = _____

        Asks questions .... 1 2 3 4 5 × _____ = _____

Active part in closing .... 1 2 3 4 5 × _____ = _____

Created a favorable impression

        Informed, prepared .... 1 2 3 4 5 × _____ = _____

        Dynamic, interested .... 1 2 3 4 5 × _____ = _____

        Listening, thinking .... 1 2 3 4 5 × _____ = _____

        A mature doer .... 1 2 3 4 5 × _____ = _____

Appearance and dress .... 1 2 3 4 5 × _____ = _____

Communication skills .... 1 2 3 4 5 × _____ = _____

Total Points _____

Comments:

Grading Scale:
    1 poor
    2 below average
    3 average
    4 above average
    5 excellent

Employment Interview Critique: Applicant Form A

Applicant _____ Critic _____

Active part in opening .... 1 2 3 4 5 × _____ = _____

Body

       Answers questions .... 1 2 3 4 5 × _____ = _____

       Asks questions .... 1 2 3 4 5 × _____ = _____

Active part in closing .... 1 2 3 4 5 × _____ = _____

Created a favorable impression

       Informed, prepared .... 1 2 3 4 5 × _____ = _____

       Dynamic, interested .... 1 2 3 4 5 × _____ = _____

       Listening, thinking .... 1 2 3 4 5 × _____ = _____

       A mature doer .... 1 2 3 4 5 × _____ = _____

Appearance and dress .... 1 2 3 4 5 × _____ = _____

Communication skills .... 1 2 3 4 5 × _____ = _____

Total Points _____

Comments:

Grading Scale:
    1 poor
    2 below average
    3 average
    4 above average
    5 excellent

Employment Interview Critique: Applicant Form B

Applicant _____ Critic _____

Opening: firm handshake, good eye contact, active participant

Points _____

Answering questions: language and grammar, to the point, thorough, honest and not evasive, evidence, reasons and not excuses, a "doer"

Points _____

Asking questions: primary questions, probing questions, phrasing of questions, avoidance of pitfalls

Points _____

Closing: active participant, what happens next, interest in the position and organization

Points _____

Created a favorable impression: appearance and dress, interest in position and organization, prepared, intelligent, well-informed, mature doer

Points _____

Communication skills: verbal, nonverbal, listening

Points _____

Total Points _____

Employment Interview Critique: Applicant Form B

Applicant _____ Critic _____

_____

Opening: firm handshake, good eye contact, active participant

Points _____

Answering questions: language and grammar, to the point, thorough, honest and not evasive, evidence, reasons and not excuses, a "doer"

Points _____

Asking questions: primary questions, probing questions, phrasing of questions, avoidance of pitfalls

Points _____

Closing: active participant, what happens next, interest in the position and organization

Points _____

Created a favorable impression: appearance and dress, interest in position and organization, prepared, intelligent, well-informed, mature doer

Points _____

Communication skills: verbal, nonverbal, listening

Points _____

Total Points _____

Employment Interview Critique: Applicant Form B

Applicant _____ Critic _____

Opening: firm handshake, good eye contact, active participant

Points _____

Answering questions: language and grammar, to the point, thorough, honest and not evasive, evidence, reasons and not excuses, a "doer"

Points _____

Asking questions: primary questions, probing questions, phrasing of questions, avoidance of pitfalls

Points _____

Closing: active participant, what happens next, interest in the position and organization

Points _____

Created a favorable impression: appearance and dress, interest in position and organization, prepared, intelligent, well-informed, mature doer

Points _____

Communication skills: verbal, nonverbal, listening

Points _____

Total Points _____

Interview Plan for the Recruiter

This guide is most appropriate for conducting interviews with applicants who are at least minimally qualified for a position with a particular organization and are aware of the basic position for which they are applying.

1. Prior to the interview review thoroughly all materials available on applicants: resume, cover letter, application form, letters of recommendation.

2. Prepare a moderate schedule of questions.

3. Prepare the information you will give about the position and your organization.

4. Choose a location and seating arrangement conducive to an effective interview interaction.

5. Create an informal, relaxed atmosphere by greeting applicants in a friendly manner and introducing yourself and your position with the organization.

6. Involve applicants in the opening.

7. Encourage applicants to speak freely and openly: (a) by telling them what to expect during the interview and (b) by starting with a few easy-to-answer, open-ended questions.

8. After applicants are relaxed and into the flow of the interview, ask challenging questions that put applicants on the job: behavioral based, current critical incident, historical critical incident, hypothetical.

9. During the body of the interview, explore and observe the applicant's:

   ☐ *Ability to communicate:* nonverbal communication, verbal communication, listening, interpersonal skills

   ☐ *Physical bearing:* poise, dynamism, dress, physical appearance

   ☐ *Maturity:* professional, personal, social

   ☐ *Motivation:* desire to enter this field or profession, interest in your organization, interest in this position, desire to achieve, evidence of being a "doer"

   ☐ *Emotional stability:* ability to handle stress and pressure, self-discipline, self-confidence, mental alertness

   ☐ *Integrity:* professional ethics, morals, sincerity, dependability, genuineness

   ☐ *Fit for this position with this organization:* experiences, training, education, knowledge, expertise, accomplishments, goals, skills, personal attributes

10. Before giving information or turning the interview over to applicants, ask two critical transition questions:

    ☐ What do you know about my organization?

    ☐ What do you know about this position?

    Answers to these questions will reveal: (a) how well applicants have done their homework, (b) the level of interest in your position and organization, and (c) what information you need to provide by knowing where the applicant's knowledge leaves off.

11. Give information about the organization and position applicants do not have or is not readily available in organizational literature or Web sites.

12. Allow adequate time for applicants to ask questions. Be specific and informative in your answers.

13. Close interviews by telling applicants what will happen next and when applicants will learn about a decision on additional interviews or about a hiring decision. Name the person applicants should contact if the need arises.

14. Involve applicants in the closing.

15. Express appreciation for the applicant's interest in your organization and position.

16. Record your impressions of the applicant immediately following each interview.

17. Make your final decision only after considering all relevant information about all applicants for a position.

18. Be certain applicants are informed of the results at the earliest possible time.

EEOC Exercise

According to EEOC guidelines and state legislation, which of the following questions are *lawful* and which are *unlawful*? If a question is generally unlawful, under what *circumstances* might they be lawful?

	Lawful	Unlawful	Circumstances
1. Have you ever been convicted of a felony?	✓		
2. Where were you born?		✓	
3. Any physical handicaps I should know about?		✓	Construction, work w/ hands, need legs.
4. Could you work the midnight to 8:00 a.m. shift?	✓		
5. How fluent are you in French?	✓		
6. Are you a beer drinker?		✓	Brewery Job, Personal preference
7. I see you're not engaged or married.		✓	Religious or Spousal counseling
8. Any grandchildren yet?		✓	Nannying?
9. Amy Chu. Is that Chinese or Korean?		✓	
10. Which religious holidays do you observe?		✓	
11. Do you consider yourself a Republican or a Democrat?		✓	Political career
12. How do you handle stress on the job?	✓		
13. Who takes care of your children?		✓	Planning for career - Time off - Exceptions for tardiness
14. Are you considering graduate school?	✓		
15. Why did you leave the military?		✓	

Recruiter Questions Exercise

Each of the following questions contains one or more common recruiter question pitfalls. Identify the pitfall(s) of each question and rewrite it to make it a good question. Avoid committing a new pitfall when rephrasing the question.

1. I'm sorry to hear that you don't have more experience. Tell me about the field project you are doing.

   Evaluated" response

   Tell me about

2. Tell me about your work in the Forest Service. Was it challenging?

   Open- Close switch

   Seperate ?'s

3. Where did you begin your college studies?

   resume question

   Don't ask

4. Do you feel qualified for the position we have open in marketing?

   Yes-No

   What makes you qualified?

5. How did you lose your left hand?

   EEO violation

6. What did your father do?

EEO violation

7. Have you checked out our Web site?

~~Evaluative Response~~

Bipolar Trap

What did you find interesting about the website

8. Did you switch majors to avoid the math requirements in economics?

~~Loaded question~~

Guessing Game

Why did you switch majors

9. I assume you can work under pressure?

·Yes-No, Leading push

Can you work under pressure

How do you work under pressure

10. Tell me about your internship at KYZ Enterprises and your summer work at Sherman's.

Double-barreled

Split ?'s

Interview Plan for the Applicant

This guide is appropriate for taking part in interviews with recruiters when you are at least minimally qualified for a position with a particular organization, are aware of the position for which you are applying, and are interested in the position.

1. Do a careful self-analysis before searching for a position.

2. Review thoroughly all materials available on the organization and position.

3. Prepare a moderate schedule of questions you will ask when given the opportunity.

4. Come to the interview with confidence in your qualifications and preparation for this position.

5. Take an active part in the opening and exhibit good interpersonal skills.

6. During the body of the interview:

   ☐ *Listen* and *think* before answering questions, particularly behavioral-based, critical incident, hypothetical, past performance, task-oriented, and problem-solving questions.

   ☐ Answer questions to the point, thoroughly, and with evidence.

   ☐ Respond carefully and tactfully to unlawful questions.

   ☐ Be honest!

   ☐ Ask mature, insightful questions that avoid common pitfalls and the "me . . . me" complex.

   ☐ Appear in manner, answers, and questions to be a *doer*.

   ☐ Attempt to show that you are a good fit for this position and organization.

7. Take an active part in the closing by discovering what will happen next and when, who you should contact if necessary, and how.

8. If appropriate, express interest in the position and organization.

9. Debrief yourself immediately after the interview, focusing on troublesome questions, your answers to questions, questions you asked, and information you did and did not obtain during the interview.

10. Write a professional thank you note.

Self-Analysis Prior to Employment Interviewing

A crucial first step in the search for a suitable position is a thorough and honest self-appraisal of who and what you have been, are, and wish to become. This analysis serves two major purposes: (1) to help you make wiser career decisions and (2) to prepare you for questions you and recruiters will ask during interviews. The checklist below provides a systematic framework for your self-analysis.

Place a checkmark along the scale that seems to describe you best at the moment or provide the requested information. Be honest in your assessment; the only person you will fool is yourself.

1. What are my *personality* strengths and weaknesses?

reliable	____	____	____	____	____	unreliable
honest	____	____	____	____	____	dishonest
high moral standards	____	____	____	____	____	low moral standards
motivated	____	____	____	____	____	unmotivated
assertive	____	____	____	____	____	acquiescent
open-minded	____	____	____	____	____	closed-minded
mature	____	____	____	____	____	immature
ambitious	____	____	____	____	____	lazy
conscientious	____	____	____	____	____	unscrupulous
emotionally in control	____	____	____	____	____	emotionally out of control
able to take criticism	____	____	____	____	____	unable to take criticism
able to work under pressure	____	____	____	____	____	unable to work under pressure

2. What are my *intellectual* strengths and weaknesses?

creative	____	____	____	____	____	uncreative
intelligent	____	____	____	____	____	unintelligent
analytical	____	____	____	____	____	nonanalytical
organized	____	____	____	____	____	disorganized
able to organize	____	____	____	____	____	unable to organize
quick learner	____	____	____	____	____	slow learner

3. What are my *communicative* strengths and weaknesses?

ability with co-workers: strong	____	____	____	____	____	weak
ability with supervisors: strong	____	____	____	____	____	weak
oral communication skills: strong	____	____	____	____	____	weak
written communication skills: strong	____	____	____	____	____	weak
ability to listen: strong	____	____	____	____	____	weak
poised	____	____	____	____	____	ill at ease
perceptive						unperceptive

4. What have been my *accomplishments* and *failures*?

	Accomplishments	**Failures**
in school:	_____	_____
	_____	_____
	_____	_____
extra-curricular:	_____	_____
	_____	_____
	_____	_____
relationships:	_____	_____
	_____	_____
	_____	_____
professional:	_____	_____
	_____	_____
	_____	_____
goals set/met:	_____	_____
	_____	_____
	_____	_____

5. What are my professional *strengths* and *weaknesses*?

	Strengths	**Weaknesses**
informal training:	_____	_____
	_____	_____
	_____	_____
formal training:	_____	_____
	_____	_____
	_____	_____
experiences:	_____	_____
	_____	_____
	_____	_____
references:	_____	_____
	_____	_____
	_____	_____
professional memberships:	_____	_____
	_____	_____
	_____	_____
talents:	_____	_____
	_____	_____

6. What are my professional *interests* and *disinterests*:

	Interests	Disinterests
areas of study:	_____	_____
new training:	_____	_____
specializations:	_____	_____
detail work:	_____	_____
administration:	_____	_____
travel:	_____	_____
relocation:	_____	_____
short-range goals:	_____	_____
long-range goals:	_____	_____

7. What do I *desire* in a position?

responsibility: important	___ ___ ___ ___ ___	unimportant
security: important	___ ___ ___ ___ ___	unimportant
contact with people: important	___ ___ ___ ___ ___	unimportant
independence: important	___ ___ ___ ___ ___	unimportant
involvement in decision making: important	___ ___ ___ ___ ___	unimportant
fringe benefits: important	___ ___ ___ ___ ___	unimportant
type of supervision: important	___ ___ ___ ___ ___	unimportant
type of co-workers: important	___ ___ ___ ___ ___	unimportant
prestige of organization: important	___ ___ ___ ___ ___	unimportant
type of work: important	___ ___ ___ ___ ___	unimportant

8. What are my *valued needs* as a human being?

possessions: high value	___ ___ ___ ___ ___	low value
salary: high value	___ ___ ___ ___ ___	low value
prestige: high value	___ ___ ___ ___ ___	low value
free time: high value	___ ___ ___ ___ ___	low value
recognition: high value	___ ___ ___ ___ ___	low value
advancement: high value	___ ___ ___ ___ ___	low value
family: high value	___ ___ ___ ___ ___	low value
lasting relationships: high value	___ ___ ___ ___ ___	low value
"roots": high value	___ ___ ___ ___ ___	low value
"success": high value	___ ___ ___ ___ ___	low value

9. Why did I *attend* the following and how *pleased* am I with this decision?

    a. _____ college/university/technical school: _____

    _____

    b. _____ college/university/technical school: _____

    _____

    c. _____ college/university/technical school: _____

    _____

10. Why did I *study* the following and *how pleased* am I with these choices?

    a. _____

    _____

    b. _____

    _____

    c. _____

    _____

11. Why did I *accept* the following positions and *how pleased* am I with these choices?

    a. _____

    _____

    b. _____

    _____

    c. _____

    _____

This checklist is based on materials in Lois J. Einhorn, *Interviewing . . . A Job In Itself* (Bloomington, IN: The Career Center, 1977); Marilyn Hutchinson and Sue E. Spooner, *Job Search Barometer* (Bethlehem, PA: The College Placement Council, 1975); and Charles J. Stewart and William B. Cash, *Interviewing: Principles and Practices* (New York: McGraw-Hill, 2009).

Cover Letter for Analysis and Criticism

This letter is being sent to a company advertising for an entry level sales position with a Midwestern seed company with locations throughout the Midwestern states from Ohio to the Dakotas. What are its strengths and weaknesses? Would you arrange for an interview with this person based on this letter? What recommendations would you make to improve this letter?

612 Burnside Road
Silver Lake, MI 48109
January 13, 2011

Personnel Office
King Seed Company
2037 Lafayette Road
New Paris, OH 45347

Dear Sir:

I am writing this letter in response to your advertisement about an entry levl position in sales. I'm interested in a sales position with a progressive company like your's that will allow me to use my education as a State Cougar and considerable experiences to advance to upper management. Their are lots of awesome things happing in agriculture today.

I will graduate this spring with a B.S. in organizational leadership and supervision. My courses and experiences have prepared me well for positions in management, accounting, training, sales, and stuff like that. Courses relevant to you position are english, public speaking, psychology, and management strategies. My work experiences and to internships have given me practical, real-world experiences. My father was in telemarketing for years in the Milwauke area.

I have always had an interest in retail management, and Cincinati is an area in which I would like to locate. I have family in that area.

Attached is a copy of my resume, and I can send additional information if you wish. I will be in your area of ohio in mid-February for a wedding (not mine), and that would be a convenient time for me to stop by to talk.

Thanks for your consideration. Hope to here from you soom.

Yours,

Thomas "Tommy" Thompson

Resume for Analysis and Criticism

This resume is being sent to a company advertising for an entry level sales position with a seed company with locations throughout the Midwestern states from Ohio to the Dakotas. What are its strengths and weaknesses? Would you arrange for an interview with this person based on this resume? What recommendations would you make to improve this resume?

Thomas "Tommy" Thompson
612 Burnside Road
Silver Lake, MI 48109
734-116-2007

Objective:
A job in management, accounting, or training with a progressive company that will enable me to use my experiences and education to advance to upper management.

Education:
Silver Lake High School, Silver Lake, Michigan, 2006
Forest River Community College, A.A., 2008
Central State University, B.S. in OLS expected spring of 2011
    G.P.A. 2.00
Selected courses: English, Public Speaking, Supervision, Human Resources, Management, Statistics, and Retail Sales

Experiences:
Silver Lake *Daily Trout*—delivery, enlarged circulation, improved on-time delivery
Grant Residence Hall—Waiter Captain, trained and supervised new waiters
Good Health Fitness—sales and management
OLS Student Association Vice President: arranged for guest speakers, presided over meetings, wrote a new constitution for the organization
Silver Lake Aquatics Center—life guard and first aid instructor

Honors and awards:
    National Honor Society, All-State in Golf, Golden Apple Society, Dean's List

Memberships: Young Republicans, National Rifle Association, Students for Life, National Tea Party

Hobbies: Woodworking, hiking, biking

References Upon Request

Resume Clinic

The purpose of this assignment is to give you an opportunity to review a number of resumes submitted by a variety of applicants for the same position to sharpen your ability to develop strong resumes during future internship and employment searches. Applicants in this assignment are applying for an introductory position in public relations with Saint Elizabeth Hospital.

The class will be divided into teams of five or six students. Each team will review the same five resumes for applicants applying for a position in public relations. The resumes are ordered alphabetically, not according to qualifications or experiences.

Each team will review the five resumes with the following criteria in mind:

1. How impressive is the career objective: precise, singular, targeted to an introductory level position in public relations? How well does the objective match with what the organization seems to be seeking?

2. How thorough are the applicant's education and training for a position in public relations: courses, GPA, degree, quality of programs and schools?

3. What experiences does this applicant have that are relevant for a position in public relations: organizational activities, internships, co-ops, volunteer positions, paid positions?

4. What are the applicant's achievements and accomplishments and what do they indicate about the applicant's potential: awards, membership in scholastic honor societies, leadership positions, promotions, assignments?

5. Is the wording positive and assertive? Does it employ action verbs and up-to-date key words the employer would be looking for in resumes?

6. Does the selected format (chronological or functional) play to the applicant's strengths as a candidate for the specific position being applied for?

7. How effective is the resume in appearance: appropriate color, uncrowded, use of font sizes, carefully blocked for ease of review and location of important information?

8. Is the resume free of errors: grammar, language, spellings, punctuation, typing?

After each team has reviewed the five resumes, it will rank order them from most to least desirable for an introductory level position in public relations. Why did the top two rise to the top of the pile? Which, if any, applicants would the team reject on the basis of the resume?

After all teams have completed their reviews and rankings, a member from each team will present and explain briefly to the class its ranking of the resumes.

Why did team and individual rankings differ?

What are subjective and objective characteristics inherent in resumes?

What have you learned about preparing your own resume from this resume clinic?

Crissey Arrington

2135 Fourth Street
Toledo, OH 43606

OBJECTIVE: Entry level position in advertising, marketing, or public relations.

EDUCATION: Bowling Green State University, Bowling Green, Ohio
B.A. Degree, Majors in Communication and Marketing
May 2011

RELATED COURSEWORK:

Presentational Speaking	Consumer Behavior
Sales & Promotion	Advertising
Introduction to Public Relations	Global Com. Networks
Interviewing Principles	Psychology of Audiences

RELATED EXPERIENCE

- Coordinated promotional campaign for Northwest Ohio Regional Health Center. Developed creative strategy, prepared radio commercials, supervised direct mail, organized recruitment activities for volunteers.

- Assisted in marketing research project for Bowling Green State University Career Center; gathered, recorded, and analyzed statistical data.

- Helped with an advertising campaign for D & C Chrysler and Dodge in Toledo, Ohio. Identified audiences, suggested strategies, and recruited college talent for the ads.

EMPLOYMENT RECORD:

6/09–Present: Night manager
Burger Barn, Bowling Green, Ohio

2006–2009: Cashier
Tom & Jerry's Silver Spoon, Maumee, Ohio

ACTIVITIES: American Marketing Association
Communication Arts Club
Rhythm on Ice Troup

REFERENCES: Available upon request.

Ashley Downing

1214 Ohio Vista Drive
Marietta, Ohio 45750
(740) 357-2056

Education

Marietta College   Marietta, Ohio
B.A. May 2011   Major: Speech Communication
                                                   Minor: Mass Media

Work Experience

Travel Agent   Summers 08, 09, 10
Northern Kentucky Travel   Covington, Kentucky

Assisted travel agents in booking educational and business tours; handled ticketing, reservations, and cancellations; and narrated travel videos during information evenings.

Sales Associate   2008-2010
College Book Store   Marietta, Ohio

Waited on customers, stocked shelves, ordered out-of-stock books, and purchased used textbook from students.

College Activities

2008	Helped to organize the Freshman Jamboree
2009	Handled Public Relations for Homecoming Activities
2010-2011	Treasurer for the Public Relations Student Society of America
2008-2010	Dean's Ambassador for the School of Arts and Sciences
Fall 2010	Study Abroad in Spain

Hobbies

Traveling, Sports, Reading, Dancing

DALE FERGUSON

135 Maple Avenue
Muncie, IN 47306
6789-6789-6789
E-mail: dferg@BSU.edu

1215 North Adams
Indianapolis, IN 46227
317-903-6647

Professional Objective: To obtain a public relations position with a dynamic and growing company.

Education: Ball State University
B.A. May 2011 – Cum Laude
Major – Communication
Grade point average – 3.65
Related course work   —   12 hours in public relations
6 hours in organizational communication
6 hours in public speaking
6 hours in advertising

Work Experience: December 2008 – Present
Free Methodist Church of Yorktown, Indiana
Communications and Development (part-time)
Responsible for writing and editing church publications, aiding the development officer in contacting past donors and potential new donors, participated in a public relations campaign to alter the image of a rural church.

June 2006 – December 2008
Triple Y Texas Barbecue, Muncie, Indiana
Assistant Manager (part-time)
Responsible for handling all money made during hours worked, open or closed the restaurant, supervised five employees on each shift.

Internships: United Way of Anderson
Boys and Girls Club of Muncie

Activities and Honors: Golden Key National Honor Society
Dean's List several semesters
Forensics Team

Comments: Willing to travel and/or relocate. A self-starter. Always give 110%

Marty Stoddard

212 Hemmingway Place
Vermillion, SD 57069
(605) 916-2693
E-mail: Mstoddard@AOL.com

Occupational Goal	Chief PR officer at a medical facility
Job Objective	Trainee in PR or advertising at a health care center with the possibility of advancement
Work Experience	**Siegfried's, Vermillion, SD, 2009-2011**
	Waited on tables, acted as assistant manager on weekends, trained new employees, made bank deposits
	Kohl's Department Store, Sioux Falls, SD, 2007-2009
	Salesperson in men's area. Promoted to Sunday and night supervisor after one year. Duties included sitting up ads and special promotions, authorizing exchanges and refunds, supervising part-time employees.
Internships	**Athletic Department, University of South Dakota,** Fall 2006
	Made recruiting calls for the Booster's Club, helped too edit and write feature stories for the Booster's Club Newsletter
	Red Cross, Vermillion, SD, Spring 2008
	Helped with mailings, created posters, worked with to corporate sponsors for blood drives
Education	**University of South Dakota**
	Bachelor of Arts in communication, June 2010
	Selected courses: Public Speaking, Organizational Communication, Interpersonal Communication, Principles of Interviewing, Communication Research Methods, Introduction to Public Relations, Practicum in Public Relations
Skills	Foreign Languages: French and German
	Programming Language: BASIC

Megan Zeller

3140 Maple
Landsdale, PA 19422
(215) 674-2044
E-mail: Mzeller@AOL.com

OBJECTIVE

Seeking a career with a progressive organization dedicated to public and community service

EDUCATION

Bachelor of Arts, June 2011, LaSalle University, Philadelphia, PA

Major: Communication
Concentration: Public Relations
Minor: English

Earned 80% of college expenses.

EXPERIENCE

Public Relations

- Helped to create student-run public relations agency
- Developed public relations plan for a community health clinic
- Assisted with development campaign for LaSalle University
- Created image pieces for a Neighborhood Watch program
- Participated in United Way campaign

Writing and Editing

- Assisted a faculty member with a professional journal
- Wrote feature articles for the student newspaper
- Wrote press releases for a congressional candidate
- Edited pieces for a compilation of short stories

WORK EXPERIENCE

2008-2011 Montgomery County Parks Department

2006-2008 Pennsylvania Turnpike Commission

2004-2008 Burger King

ACTIVITIES

Public Relations Student Society of America
Intramural sports
Habitat for Humanity

Responses to Recruiter Questions

Write an answer to each of the following questions a recruiter might ask you to answer during an interview. Review guidelines for answering questions effectively. Make your answer reflect your true education, experiences, feelings, attitudes, and interests.

1. Tell me about a time when you had to meet an almost impossible deadline for a project and how you handled it.

    St. F's Michelle Jewell interview.

2. Last year we had to downsize our engineering department because of the severe economic recession. If you had been with us, how would you have made the cuts in staff?

    I would have made them bases off of performance

3. Suppose you came across two production workers who were in a near-violent argument. What would you do?

    Intervene; seperate the parties; try to calm them down. later on meet w/ each of them either together or seperate. find out the issue, ; find ways to resolve it.

4. Here is a book on how to coach employees to enhance their careers. Why should I buy it from you?

    Because its the best DAMN Book out there for this Stuff.

5. If you were a fruit, what kind of fruit would you be?

    ~~I would be a blackberry~~

    Concise answer you can believe in

Responses to Unlawful Questions

Each of the following questions violates an EEO law but continues to appear in many employment interviews. They pose serious dilemmas for applicants. Explain why each question is unlawful and then provide an answer you might give to your advantage.

1. Does your helper dog go everywhere with you?

   Unlawful because: Illudes to a disability *personal*

   Your response: I do use the dog, but I am able to do things on my own

2. Ashanti. What nationality is that?

   Unlawful because: Race/cultural background

   Your response: Why is that related to the job?

3. Do you consider yourself to be a religious person?

   Unlawful because: Religion

   Your response: • By law, I don't have to answer that.
   • I don't feel comfortable
   • I'm an Ethical person.

4. What do you think of the Tea Party Movement?

   Unlawful because: Political

   Your response: ∅

5. (Asked of a male with gray hair) How long would you expect to work for us?

   Unlawful because: Age discrimination

   Your response: ~~thee~~

6. Do you plan to have children?

   Unlawful because: _Personal_

   Your response:

7. What would you do if your husband was asked to transfer?

   Unlawful because: _Personal_

   Your response:

8. (Asked of a male applying for a position as a flight attendant) Why did you decide to enter a field traditionally populated by females?

   Unlawful because: _Gender_

   Your response:

9. Many of our supervisors are in their sixties. How would you feel about working for a much older person?

   Unlawful because: _Age_

   Your response:

10. I see you went to a traditionally all-Black college?

    Unlawful because: _Race_

    Your response:

Applicant Questions Exercise

Each of the following questions contains one or more common applicant question pitfalls: have to, typology, little bitty, pleading, immature, double-barreled, leading push, yes (no) response, bipolar trap, guessing game, and open-to-closed switch. Identify the pitfall(s) of each question and rephrase it to make it a good question. *Avoid committing a new pitfall when rephrasing a question.*

1. Do you have a policy for unexcused absences?

2. Do you like to work for this company?

3. Tell me a little bit about your operation in Toronto.

4. Would I have to travel much?

5. Is there a typical work day?

6. Did you close your plant in Michigan because it was unionized?

7. Tell me about your stock sharing plan and your 401K program.

8. What type of performance review do you employ?

9. I assume you promote employees primarily according to their performance?

10. Tell me about your new strategic plan; does it address research as well as marketing goals?

Applicant Question Schedule Exercise

Listed below are two schedules of questions applicants might use during employment interviews. What "image" does each schedule communicate? What image would you prefer to communicate as an applicant? How might you change each schedule? Which questions, if any, would you delete? How might you combine the schedules? If you were an employer, which applicant would you choose if the decision came down to the applicant's questions?

Schedule A

1. What is the usual salary range for someone with my background?

2. What major benefits does your organization offer its employees?

3. What are my chances for advancement with your organization?

4. What kind of support would I have for continuing my education?

5. Other than money, what kinds of rewards could I expect from your organization?

6. How does your organization pay relocation expenses?

Schedule B

1. What, in your estimation, is the most unique characteristic of your organization?

2. How are teams employed in your organization?

3. What would my supervisor expect of me during my probationary period with your organization?

4. How might an advanced degree affect my stature in your organization?

5. What is your organization's notion of an ideal employee?

6. What kinds of tasks would I perform during a typical day as a _____ with your organization?

Employment Interview for Review and Analysis

This screening interview took place in the Center for Career Opportunities at Purdue University between an undergraduate student in agricultural economics and a representative of a large agricultural chemical manufacturer. Only the names and minor details have been changed in this transcript. Analyze this interview by using the critique forms provided in this unit.

☐ How effective is the opening for recruiter and applicant?

☐ How effective is the opening question and the applicant's response?

☐ How effective are the recruiter's and applicant's questions?

☐ How effective are the recruiter's and applicant's answers?

☐ How effectively do the recruiter and applicant probe into answers?

☐ How effective is the recruiter's information giving?

☐ How effective is the overall structure of the interview?

☐ How effective are the recruiter's and applicant's verbal skills?

☐ How effectively do the recruiter and applicant listen to one another?

☐ How effective is the closing for recruiter and applicant?

1. **Employer:** Steve Johnson?

2. **Applicant:** Yes, Mr. Carpenter?

3. **Employer:** Come in. Please sit down. Would you like a cup of coffee?

4. **Applicant:** No, thank you.

5. **Employer:** Steve, would you tell me something about yourself, your background, etc.?

6. **Applicant:** Okay. I live down in southern Indiana, very near New Albany. I live on a farm and my father raises dairy cows, some hogs, corn, and wheat. I went to school at a very small high school. We had only 89 in my graduating class.

7. **Employer:** Tell me how you decided to study ag. econ.

8. **Applicant:** I decided to study ag. econ. as a senior in high school. As a freshman and sophomore I wanted to go into engineering, and I chose Purdue as the logical choice. I didn't want to pay out-of-state tuition, so here I am.

9. **Employer:** Tell me what interested you in sales. Why that over another job?

10. **Applicant:** First of all, here at Purdue we have a very fine ag. econ. department. In my association with the professors they tell me about the kinds of jobs available and the rewards of each and the returns for each. They stress the fact that most managers come from the sales department. In other words, this is the proving ground.

11. **Employer:** Tell me why you chose sales.

12. **Applicant:** Well, for myself, I like a competitive job, and sales is just that. I like being rewarded according to my efforts, and sales is the place to do it.

13. **Employer:** Outside of gratifications of the job what do you envision a sales job would be like?

14. **Applicant:** What I think is important is the product. I like to have a product worthwhile being sold and a good application. I would want to sell some thing with a real and definite purpose. I feel that a sales job has to do with contacting people and showing them a product that they can use to their own advantage.

15. **Employer:** What about the future, do you look at sales as a stepping stone, or as a career? Tell me about your future plans.

16. **Applicant:** So far as the future, I feel that it would be a step to the key management positions. I would look forward to a management position after proving myself in sales.

17. **Employer:** By the way, along with ag. econ., do you have a minor?

18. **Applicant:** I don't have as far as I can see. I have a good background in chemistry, math, and about the same in English, psychology, and philosophy so I can't really say.

19. **Employer:** Would you say you lean towards some part of agriculture?

20. **Applicant:** Do you mean agronomy, animal science, etc.?

21. **Employer:** Yes.

22. **Applicant:** I lean a little towards animal science, but my interest sort of is in finance.

23. **Employer:** Sounds like a good minor to me! Maybe I should talk about the job we have, and this will guide our discussion. Agri-Chem is a manufacturing company for agricultural chemicals such as fertilizer, herbicides, and blasting agents. We have our own pesticides, etc. I don't know how familiar you are with these. We sell these products nationally. We have four ways to market these. First, national accounts such as Armour who is a national distributor. Second, another form is through the distributor. We call a distributor someone less than national. Third, another way is through co-ops and anyone who sells to farmers. Fourth, another way is through our farm service centers. Are you familiar with these farm service centers?

24. **Applicant:** Yes, I believe I am.

25. **Employer:** These centers have storage areas for fertilizers and chemicals. We also offer another service to farmers. After testing their soil, we custom mix fertilizers for them. Also we sell anhydrous ammonia and liquid fertilizer. The idea is to offer a total fertilizer program. We want to help the farmer increase his profits as well as ours. Another idea is to give the farmer more service. The trend is toward bigger farms, and these farmers cannot keep up with the technology and evaluate all of the different products. So we try to provide the technology he wants and to show him we can provide him with what he needs. Now, is this the kind of area of sales you would be interested in? Is this the product line you are interested in? Sometimes I find that people are more interested in product lines.

26. **Applicant:** I would be familiar with what you have to sell and know the application. I can budget out whether it would be profitable, etc. I am familiar with your products.

27. **Employer:** Some people have a preference for selling direct to farmers. Others are against it and would rather sell to distributors.

28. **Applicant:** I would like to do that if I have a good product to sell. I've seen a lot of salesmen, and some just try to sell some small product which doesn't amount to much. I would want to sell a product that has an application and not just some gimmick. I want to tell a man something and, barring other factors, it would do just what I said it would do.

29. **Employer:** Do you mean factors like it not raining or something?

30. **Applicant:** Yes. I would like to talk to farmers and feel I can pick out those who would buy what I have to sell. I can talk to farmers all day because I know them. I could pick the interested man.

31. **Employer:** How do you feel about relocation and things like that?

32. **Applicant:** I put on the form that I would like the Midwest, but I think I would like to travel around. I haven't traveled much at all.

33. **Employer:** Why would you feel you wouldn't want to work in the South? Is it because you are not familiar with that part of the country?

34. **Applicant:** Well I don't know. From a lot of what I have seen and heard, it's so hot and if I could say something, I would rather work up here in the Midwest.

35. **Employer:** Well, you're more familiar with the products up here and probably wouldn't know too much about cotton and peanuts. I think that I'd like you to come to Kansas City for some interviews. Does that sound okay to you?

36. **Applicant:** Yes, it does. It sounds good from your point of view and from mine.

37. **Employer:** I think I have given you a brief introduction of what we have to offer, but there are a lot of positions available that are similar. I would like to talk to you in depth and tell you what working for us is like and give you an opportunity to talk with some of our people. Now, do you have any questions for me about the job?

38. **Applicant:** As far as the job, I wanted to know what kind of job it is—house-to-house or what, but you've told me that. Let me ask you this about the salary. Do you pay on commission or how do you do that?

39. **Employer:** All our people are on straight salary. Salaries vary, and we would make you an offer. You can accept or reject that offer. There are a lot of pros and cons to this. We pay a person for performance. One person could make more than another just by having a better territory.

40. **Applicant:** Suppose I were working for you and went out and sold a lot. How would you take this into account? Would I advance faster?

41. **Employer:** This most certainly would be taken into account. This provides us with some guidelines as to how to promote. We pay more for a better job.

42. **Applicant:** So far as hours of work, do you check in the morning and go from there, or are you on your own?

43. **Employer:** This is a very big point. This is probably the downfall of many sales people because they don't use their time effectively. You have a great deal of independence, and it takes a great deal of maturity and self-dependence. Well, that's all I have, and I thank you for coming in. I'll get in touch with you early next week.

chapter
four

Persuasive Interviewing

Persuasive Interview Assignment

During the first several weeks of this course, we have emphasized getting and giving information as accurately and completely as possible. We have noted the danger of interviewer bias in questions, manner, and appearance. This assignment switches gears from the goals of neutrality and objectivity to the goal of influencing an interviewee's way of thinking, feeling, or acting. You are more likely to achieve such common interview goals as selling, buying, recruiting, seeking employment, altering behaviors, and motivating if you adapt to the other party and situation, are thoroughly prepared, and conduct a well-structured interview.

The purpose of this assignment is to give you an experience in analyzing an interviewee, researching a topic, structuring a need-solution interview, and adapting evidence, appeals, strategies, and tactics to a specific interviewee in a specific situation. Role playing is the most common and effective way to teach and learn these skills. We will provide you with adequate opportunities to make this assignment as realistic and relevant as possible but, as in "real life," you will need to take on roles that are challenging and unexpected. We "play" a wide variety of roles every day.

Instructions for Interviewers

1. You have three options when selecting a case for this assignment: (a) select a persuasion case from your textbook or this text, (b) modify a case found in the textbook or this text so it is more relevant and interesting to you, or (c) create a case of your own to make this a valuable experience for you. If you modify

a case or create one of your own, please submit a draft of this case to your instructor for approval by _____. Option b and c cases must be of the same level of difficulty as ones provided in your textbook and this text.

2. Complete the **Persuasive Interview Preparation Report** and submit it to your instructor by

    _____.

3. Structure your persuasive interview according to the outline in your textbook. Be sure to adapt to the interviewee and the situation. A question schedule will not work as a structure for this assignment.

4. Use the real names and genders of both parties during interviews, not the ones that might appear in some printed cases.

5. Involve your interviewee in the interview. Do not merely give a speech to an audience of one. Interviewees will play the roles as described in each case and will not remain silent during interviews.

6. Create realistic evidence and documentation to support your need and solution. Develop the types of evidence that would be ideal to have for this interview and situation.

7. Employ visual aids (charts, pictures, graphs, models, objects, letters, reports, printouts, surveys) whenever possible to clarify and support your arguments and solution.

8. Your instructor may select different options for this interview assignment.

    Option A: In this option, you will have _____ minutes to present a need and _____ minutes to present a solution. When the instructor says to move to the solution phase, assume that the need has been agreed to and begin with criteria any solution should meet. When the instructor calls time, stop the interview without a closing.

    Option B: In this option, you will take part in two interviews. During the first interview, you will have _____ minutes to begin developing a need. The interview will end when your instructor says to stop. During the second interview, you will have _____ minutes to begin developing a solution. We say *begin* because the cases are too complex to establish a need or present a detailed solution in the time allotted.

    Option C: In this option, you will decide whether to focus on the need or the solution phase of an interview. You will have __7-8__ minutes to develop a need or solution. If you select to focus on the solution phase, assume that a need was agreed to during an initial interview. Begin with a summary of the need and then move to criteria any solution should meet. The interview will end when your instructor says to stop.

9. Your interview will be worth a possible _____ points. Since you will not have enough time to present a complete need or solution, you will be graded on the quality of what you accomplish in the time allotted, not on how far you get.

Instructions for Interviewees

1. Study your case and role thoroughly. It is important that you play the role to challenge your interviewer to adapt to you and to meet objections.

2. Take an active part in the interview. Do not be a passive listener.

3. Challenge evidence if it seems unrealistic or irrelevant. Ask for documentation of statistics and quotations.

4. Be a critical thinker. Listen to the arguments being presented for a need and determine if you agree with the conclusions or claims made and how the interviewer reached them.

5. Insist on criteria for evaluating solutions and then apply these criteria to the recommended solution.

6. Ask for details of the proposed solution.

7. Your role in the interview will be worth a possible _____ points.

Persuasion Role Playing Cases

The Athletic Boosters Club

The persuader (age 25) is in the Office of Intercollegiate Sports at _____ and hopes to convince the interviewee to join the Athletic Boosters Club—a club that supports intercollegiate athletics through its attendance at games, help with recruitment, and financial contributions. The persuader has invited the interviewee to tour the new Aquatics Center after sending promotional materials on the Athletic Boosters Club. Rising costs of intercollegiate athletics make it necessary to enlarge the Boosters Club membership. Nonmembers who have coveted season basketball tickets may lose their good reserved seats or not be able to get tickets if they do not join because priority will be given to Club members.

The interviewee is 30 years old, attends a number of _____ athletic and musical events each year, and has had season basketball tickets since he/she was a first year undergraduate 12 years ago. In addition to a B.S. from _____, the interviewee has earned an M.A. from Saint Louis University and an M.B.A. from Northwestern University. Frequent appeals for money come from all three schools. The interviewee tends to be closed-minded and authoritarian but more optimistic than pessimistic, likes sports of all kinds, and sees the interviewer as pleasant, intelligent, and sold on _____. However, the interviewee is also aware of the possible threat to nonmember basketball season ticket holders, particularly those who have supported "minor" sports and a losing football program for many years. Loyalty will be a major value addressed by both parties during the interview.

Selling a Life Insurance Policy

The interviewer (age 24) is a sales representative for Eastern Fire and Casualty Company and would like to sell a life insurance policy to the interviewee, a casual acquaintance from the First Methodist Church near campus. The interview will take place in the interviewee's apartment.

The interviewee is 26 years old, apparently in good health, and highly intelligent. After attending college for one year, the interviewee began working as a sales representative for Mid-Atlantic Roofing and Siding. She/he decided five years later to return to college and work toward a degree in history with the goal of teaching in high school. The interviewee is now a junior at _____ and is an active student-member of the State Teachers Association and the National Education Association. The interviewee works part time at a department store and shares an apartment with a friend from Mid-Atlantic Roofing and Siding. Money is tight with school and other expenses. The interviewee is usually optimistic, but a bit suspicious of sales people, is more open than closed-minded, and holds middle American values. However, the interviewee believes that people tend to be over-insured. The interviewer is seen as young, inexperienced, and anxious to establish herself/himself with Eastern Fire and Casualty, perceived by the interviewee to be a small, local outfit.

Altering Grievance Procedures

The interviewer is 21 years old and President of the Student Government at _____. The Student Affairs Committee, of which the interviewer is a member, is considering a proposal to make major changes in student grievance procedures first developed during the 1960s. The interviewer feels strongly that changes are needed to address contemporary problems not considered when the procedures were first developed and a growing number of appeals of Grievance Committee decisions by students who have had cases come before the Committee. The interviewer hopes to convince the Dean of Students to support changes she/he is proposing to the Student Affairs Committee.

The interviewee is 45 years old and has been Dean of Students for three years. The interviewee is quite proud of changes made in the Dean's office and its supportive climate fostered with students. The interviewee tends to be friendly, cautious, and a stickler for facts above emotions. At this time, the interviewee sees no need for major changes in the current system and feels that changes in faculty and student attitudes would resolve most difficulties attributed to the system. The interviewer and interviewee have worked well together on a variety of projects since the interviewer became the President of the Student Government.

A New Computer System

After selling and servicing computer systems for 15 years, the interviewer became a convert to a new Millennium series including its unique software and is now attempting to sell the new system to long-time clients. The interviewee is founder and President of The Bargain Hunter, a company that produces a weekly publication that contains hundreds of ads and coupons for local companies and distributors. The interviewer wants to convince the interviewee that the new Millennium system has major advantages over the system used at The Bargain Hunter.

The interviewee is a highly intelligent, innovative, and educated businessperson and very active in business and professional organizations. She/he is married, conservative, believes in "success" values associated with the "American way," and open-minded. The interviewee is happy with the Apple system used for years at The Bargain Hunter and feels everyone knows the system very well. Why bring in a totally new system that may be unproven and require extensive training and possible "down-time?" The interviewee sees the interviewer as bright, friendly, and honest but a little pushy. The interviewer appears to be a dedicated convert to the new system.

A Post-Surgery Counseling Program

The interviewer is an RN and supervisor of the post-surgery recovery area at Saint Anthony's Hospital. For a number of years, the interviewer has been concerned about the lack of counseling available for patients in the hours and days following both minor and major surgical procedures. Surgeons, family physicians, and RNs have very limited time to spend with individual patients, particularly if a patient seems to be recovering "normally." The interviewer has discovered that a great many patients have questions and concerns, leave the hospital with too little or erroneous information about what they can and cannot do during recovery, and often grow angry at attendants and LPNs who are not allowed to give information or do not have the expertise to answer questions properly.

The interviewer has decided to take the need and a solution to the head of surgery at Saint Anthony's. The solution is the creation of a volunteer force of post-surgery counselors. The major hurdle the interviewer faces, beyond establishing a need, is that the head of surgery believes in a strict hierarchy among hospital staff. Physicians are in charge; RNs must not "play doctor"; LPNs must stay in their place; and others are to be seen but not heard. The interviewee is a person of few words and strictly "no-nonsense." Platitudes and generalities will be dismissed quickly. Her/his time must not be wasted on frivolous matters. And the interviewee often describes adult patients as children.

Lawn Service

The interviewer operates a franchise for Global Lawn Care in Winter Pass, California. Global Lawn Care installs sprinkler systems, mows lawns, prunes trees and bushes, and makes applications of fertilizers and herbicides. Before taking over this franchise two years ago, the previous operator had lost most of the customer base through poor management and poor service to homeowners. When the current owner-operator took over the franchise, he/she thought old customers would return because of Global's national advertising campaigns and range of services. Few have returned, and the owner-operator is now interviewing former customers to persuade them to return to Global Lawn Care. The interview will take place at the former customer's home on Hilltop Drive.

The interviewee, a retired Air Force colonel, used Global Lawn Care for nearly six years but became very angry over shoddy applications of fertilizers, ineffective herbicides, and the constant high-pressure sales calls to take more and more services. When two recent graduates of the University of California at Davis started a lawn care service called Beautiful Vistas three years ago, the interviewee contracted with them to take over the service from Global. The interviewee has been very pleased with what they have done and appreciates the lack of high-pressure sales pitches. He tells them what he wants done and when. The interviewee tends to be a loyal customer.

An Organic Farming Operation

The interviewer (age 23) graduated in agronomy last year and has traveled the country since, visiting and interviewing with owners and managers of organic farm operations. He believes this is "the wave of the future" that will prove profitable for farmers and healthful for consumers. Upon returning to his home state of Alabama, he began a campaign funded by Organic Farming of America (an organization of private and corporate farmers) to persuade farmers to convert from traditional farming with extensive use of pesticides and herbicides to purely organic operations.

The interviewee is 46 years old and a graduate of Alabama A & M. She and her husband raise sweet corn, sweet potatoes, peanuts, and a variety of melons on some 650 acres of river bottom land. Their primary customers, in addition to a roadside operation, are supermarkets in Alabama and Georgia. Low prices for produce, growing competition from other states and Mexico, and rising cost of pesticides and herbicides have required them to take positions at an auto assembly plant in Atlanta, about an hour drive from their farm. They heard the interviewer speak at a Farm Bureau meeting several weeks ago and invited him to visit with them. They see the interviewer as very young, long on formal education but short on real-world experience, and a true believer for his "cause." They are afraid the cause is more of a fad than a wave.

An Italian Restaurant Franchise

The interviewer (age 30) works for Mama Maria's, an Italian restaurant franchise located in Philadelphia. The chain is expanding into the Midwest, and the interviewer's position requires her to recruit new franchise operators. Her contacts are generated from Internet messages to restaurant owners, mailings to members of restaurant managers associations, and replies to the company's Web site. Prime targets are private restaurants facing competition from new franchise operations with large advertising budgets and the buying power of chain operations.

The interviewee (age 25) will soon inherit the family restaurant, Joe's City Café. The problem is growing competition from franchise operations such as The Texas Road House, O'Charley's, Olive Garden, Applebee's, and Outback Steakhouse. Joe's has been in the family for two generations, founded by his grandfather in 1932, and the interviewee does not want to become merely a franchisee with little control over operations, menu, ingredients, atmosphere, and purchasing. Nor does he want to lose the family business. He feels it's a good idea to talk to the interviewer, even if it's only to learn more about the franchise operations he is facing. The interviewee knows that the interviewer's job is to convert people into operators of Mama Maria's.

Sample

Persuasive Interview Preparation Report Form

Name _____

The interviewer is a sales representative for Sherman Meadows, a new housing development on 50 acres of rolling land about ten miles from town. She met the interviewees (husband and wife) at a home trade show a few months ago and feels they might be interested in a new home. Sales have been slow for several months, but interest rates are beginning to fall and more new homes are available for first-time buyers.

The interviewees are both young teachers at the local high school, with a combined income of $66,000. They have no children but plan to begin a family as soon as both of them receive tenure in 2–3 years. They are currently renting a small, two-bedroom town house a few blocks from the high school and like the location's closeness to their work. They thought about purchasing a larger home but became discouraged because of the high cost of homes, relatively high interest rates, and increased travel expenses and time that would result from any move. They see the interviewer as pleasant but a "typical" real estate sales representative who is eager to make a sale, particularly since home sales have been slow in the area for several months.

What are the most important *personal characteristics/attitudes* of the interviewee?

They would like to move to a home of their own and one that would provide space for the family they hope to start soon. Their income is modest, and they are concerned about gaining tenure in their teaching positions before jumping into larger house payments or facing the possibility of having to sell a home if one or both do not get tenure. They see the interviewer as a typical sales representative who is very eager to make a sale.

What are the major *advantages* of the persuasive situation?

The interviewees would like to have a home of their own that would be large enough for the family they plan to begin as soon as possible. Interest rates are beginning to fall, so the interviewees' salary would be less of a factor. And more homes are available than a few months ago.

What are the major *disadvantages* of the persuasive situation?

The interviewees are untenured and like the closeness of their present rental town house. They are not in favor of moving several miles from school. Their income is modest, particularly when children come along.

DEVELOPMENT OF A NEED: List in order of importance the problems/reasons why this interviewee needs to change and the sources/types of evidence you will use for each.

Problem/Reason	Source/Type of Evidence
1. Interest rates are coming down but may not stay down very long.	1. Bank rate materials and business section news items on falling interest rates.
2. The amount of mortgage money available is at a five-year high.	2. *Wall Street Journal, Business Week,* bank newsletter.
3. New moderate-priced homes may not be available in 4–5 years.	3. Sales figures on how quickly lots are selling and reports on limited new housing.

List the *criteria* any solution must meet for this interviewee in this situation.

1. Cost of homes

2. Size of homes

3. Travel ease and time

4. Resale of homes

List the details of the *solution* that best meet the criteria listed above.

1. Homes in this area range in price from $70,000–$95,000.

2. Three- and four-bedroom models range from 1,900–3,000 square feet.

3. This housing division is located on a new throughway that makes travel to the high school easy and fast.

4. Travel ease and time are superior to any other housing area with homes in preferred price range and size.

5. Data on resale of homes in this division, including time to sell and prices accepted, are some of the best in the area.

What *visual aids* will you use while establishing the need and the solution?

1. Bar graphs on trends in new housing interest rates

2. Maps of city and county showing the location of the housing division and the new throughway

3. Newspaper clippings on housing costs, interest rates, and the new throughway

4. Map of the housing division and available homes and lots for building

5. Pictures of several homes already built and for sale

6. Floor plans available that would meet the interviewees' needs

Persuasive Interview Critique: Interviewer Form A

Interviewer _____   Critic _____

Opening . . . . 1 2 3 4 5 × _____ = _____

Creating a need or desire . . . . 1 2 3 4 5 × _____ = _____

Establishing criteria . . . . 1 2 3 4 5 × _____ = _____

Presenting a solution . . . . 1 2 3 4 5 × _____ = _____

Closing . . . . 1 2 3 4 5 × _____ = _____

Evidence for need/solution . . . . 1 2 3 4 5 × _____ = _____

Effective use of visual aids . . . . 1 2 3 4 5 × _____ = _____

Answers questions and objections . . . . 1 2 3 4 5 × _____ = _____

Obtains agreements . . . . 1 2 3 4 5 × _____ = _____

Adapts to this interviewee . . . . 1 2 3 4 5 × _____ = _____

Adapts to this situation . . . . 1 2 3 4 5 × _____ = _____

Involves the interviewee . . . . 1 2 3 4 5 × _____ = _____

Communication skills . . . . 1 2 3 4 5 × _____ = _____

Total Points _____

Comments:

Grading Scale:
1 poor
2 below average
3 average
4 above average
5 excellent

Persuasive Interview Critique: Interviewer Form A

Interviewer _____   Critic _____

Opening   1   2   3   4   5   × _____ = _____

Creating a need or desire   1   2   3   4   5   × _____ = _____

Establishing criteria   1   2   3   4   5   × _____ = _____

Presenting a solution   1   2   3   4   5   × _____ = _____

Closing   1   2   3   4   5   × _____ = _____

Evidence for need/solution   1   2   3   4   5   × _____ = _____

Effective use of visual aids   1   2   3   4   5   × _____ = _____

Answers questions and objections   1   2   3   4   5   × _____ = _____

Obtains agreements   1   2   3   4   5   × _____ = _____

Adapts to this interviewee   1   2   3   4   5   × _____ = _____

Adapts to this situation   1   2   3   4   5   × _____ = _____

Involves the interviewee   1   2   3   4   5   × _____ = _____

Communication skills   1   2   3   4   5   × _____ = _____

Total Points _____

Comments:

Grading Scale:
    1 poor
    2 below average
    3 average
    4 above average
    5 excellent

Persuasive Interview Critique: Interviewer Form B

Interviewer _____ Critic _____

Opening: gains attention/interest, builds rapport, opening technique(s), involves the interviewee

Points _____

Creating a need or desire: reasoning, evidence, audio/visual aids, adapts to interviewee, use of questions, answers questions, involves the interviewee

Points _____

Establishing criteria: clearly stated, adapts to interviewee, involves the interviewee

Points _____

Presenting a solution: detailed explanation, uses criteria, meets objections, adapts to interviewee, uses audio/visual aids, involves the interviewee

Points _____

Communication skills: verbal, nonverbal, listening

Points _____

Closing: trial closing, contract/agreement, leave taking, involves the interviewee

Points _____

Total Points _____

Persuasive Interview Critique: Interviewer Form B

Interviewer _____ Critic _____

Opening: gains attention/interest, builds rapport, opening technique(s), involves the interviewee

Points _____

Creating a need or desire: reasoning, evidence, audio/visual aids, adapts to interviewee, use of questions, answers questions, involves the interviewee

Points _____

Establishing criteria: clearly stated, adapts to interviewee, involves the interviewee

Points _____

Presenting a solution: detailed explanation, uses criteria, meets objections, adapts to interviewee, uses audio/visual aids, involves the interviewee

Points _____

Communication skills: verbal, nonverbal, listening

Points _____

Closing: trial closing, contract/agreement, leave taking, involves the interviewee

Points _____

Total Points _____

Persuasive Interview Critique: Interviewer Form B

Interviewer _____ Critic _____

_____

Opening: gains attention/interest, builds rapport, opening technique(s), involves the interviewee

Points _____

_____

Creating a need or desire: reasoning, evidence, audio/visual aids, adapts to interviewee, use of questions, answers questions, involves the interviewee

Points _____

_____

Establishing criteria: clearly stated, adapts to interviewee, involves the interviewee

Points _____

_____

Presenting a solution: detailed explanation, uses criteria, meets objections, adapts to interviewee, uses audio/visual aids, involves the interviewee

Points _____

_____

Communication skills: verbal, nonverbal, listening

Points _____

_____

Closing: trial closing, contract/agreement, leave taking, involves the interviewee

Points _____

_____

Total Points _____

Persuasive Interview Critique: Interviewee Form A

Interviewee _____ Critic _____

Takes an active part in the opening . . . . 1 2 3 4 5 × _____ = _____

Plays the role of this interviewee realistically . . . . 1 2 3 4 5 × _____ = _____

Is a critical, inquisitive interviewee . . . . 1 2 3 4 5 × _____ = _____

Uses questions effectively . . . . 1 2 3 4 5 × _____ = _____

Forces interviewer to be systematic
when necessary . . . . 1 2 3 4 5 × _____ = _____

Takes an active part in the closing . . . . 1 2 3 4 5 × _____ = _____

Communication skills . . . . 1 2 3 4 5 × _____ = _____

Total Points _____

Comments:

Grading Scale:
1 poor
2 below average
3 average
4 above average
5 excellent

Persuasive Interview Critique: Interviewee Form A

Interviewee _____ Critic _____

Takes an active part in the opening . . . . 1 2 3 4 5 × _____ = _____

Plays the role of this interviewee realistically . . . . 1 2 3 4 5 × _____ = _____

Is a critical, inquisitive interviewee . . . . 1 2 3 4 5 × _____ = _____

Uses questions effectively . . . . 1 2 3 4 5 × _____ = _____

Forces interviewer to be systematic
when necessary . . . . 1 2 3 4 5 × _____ = _____

Takes an active part in the closing . . . . 1 2 3 4 5 × _____ = _____

Communication skills . . . . 1 2 3 4 5 × _____ = _____

Total Points _____

Comments:

Grading Scale:
1 poor
2 below average
3 average
4 above average
5 excellent

Persuasive Interview Critique: Interviewee Form B

Interviewee _____ Critic _____

_____

Plays the role of interviewee realistically

Points _____

Critical consumer: questions reasoning, evidence, criteria, solution

Points _____

Use of questions: appropriate, timely, mature

Points _____

Forces interviewer to be systematic when necessary

Points _____

Communication skills: verbal, nonverbal, listening

Points _____

Total Points _____

Persuasive Interview Critique: Interviewee Form B

Interviewee _____ Critic _____

Plays the role of interviewee realistically

Points _____

Critical consumer: questions reasoning, evidence, criteria, solution

Points _____

Use of questions: appropriate, timely, mature

Points _____

Forces interviewer to be systematic when necessary

Points _____

Communication skills: verbal, nonverbal, listening

Points _____

Total Points _____

Persuasive Interview Critique: Interviewee Form B

Interviewee _____ Critic _____

_____

Plays the role of interviewee realistically

Points _____

Critical consumer: questions reasoning, evidence, criteria, solution

Points _____

Use of questions: appropriate, timely, mature

Points _____

Forces interviewer to be systematic when necessary

Points _____

Communication skills: verbal, nonverbal, listening

Points _____

Total Points _____

Persuasive Interview for Review and Analysis

This interview is taking place between Alice Jones and Marcia Kent, two lifelong friends, who have organized joint-family vacations along the Atlantic coast for the past nine years. They have selected locations where condos were available for rent on the beach, a major city nearby for sightseeing and restaurants, and with a selection of excellent golf courses. For the past five summers, the two families, their children, and their grandchildren have vacationed on Ocean Isle Beach midway between Myrtle Beach, South Carolina and Wilmington, North Carolina. They have placed $150.00 deposits on four condos for next summer. Alice wants to persuade Marcia that they should go on an ocean cruise instead. Marcia likes Alice a great deal but sees her as prone to snap decisions when influenced by others.

Select A or B **Persuasive Interview Critique Forms** and do a thorough analysis of the interviewer and interviewee in this interview. Pay particular attention to how well the interviewer adapts to the interviewee and the situation and how well the interviewee plays the role of critical consumer.

1. **Interviewer:** Hi! Got a few minutes Marcia?

2. **Interviewee:** Sure. We're going out for dinner this evening because Paul is working late.

3. **Interviewer:** Great! I've been thinking about our plans for next summer's vacation on Ocean Isle.

4. **Interviewee:** Me too. I think it's this cold and gloomy weather. The beach and warm sun sound wonderful at this time of year.

5. **Interviewer:** Yeah. Well . . . I've been thinking that we might do *something* else?

6. **Interviewee:** Something else? You've been excited about returning to Ocean Isle and even talked about which golf courses you want to play this year, especially the new Cover Lake course.

7. **Interviewer:** Yeah, I know. It just seems like maybe it's time for a change, time to do something really different, a change of scenery, a new adventure.

8. **Interviewee:** A change of scenery? But we've already made deposits on four condos, a total of $600.00, and no beach is better in the area. The sunrises and sunsets are fantastic.

9. **Interviewer:** I know we have, and I've enjoyed doing all there is to do at Ocean Isle. I have talked to several people at the office who have taken ocean cruises, and they've had fantastic times.

10. **Interviewee:** An ocean cruise!

11. **Interviewer:** Yes, a cruise. Doesn't that sound exciting? The ships have great rooms, wonderful food, swimming pools, Las Vegas style entertainment, lots of games and activities, great shopping at island stops, and . . .

12. **Interviewee:** Alice! We're talking about big money here and travel problems for our children who live in Philadelphia and Chicago. Most cruise ships leave from the Miami area a long way from Ocean Isle. And what about your kids in Little Rock and Louisville?

13. **Interviewer:** Well, the cost might be a *bit* more, but it includes everything. The kids could fly down to Miami.

14. **Interviewee:** A *bit more!* Our son Greg has four children, and airline tickets for six people would be astronomical. Then what would little children do on a cruise ship? I would be scared to death they might fall overboard. I can't imagine our grandchildren in a Las Vegas nightclub setting. And wouldn't they be bored to death on a ship all day?

15. **Interviewer:** Kyle, Peggy, and Dick at the office have all gone on cruises with their children and claim there's nothing like it. Their children really love it.

16. **Interviewee:** As I recall, we followed the advice of Kyle, Peggy, and Dick before and lived to regret it. They have strange notions of what is fun, and do not have small children.

17. **Interviewer:** Well, that's true for a couple of times, but they were correct about the resort in the Smokey Mountains. And they saw all of the activities for children on their cruise ships.

18. **Interviewee:** Yes, they were correct *once*. I think our families need to sit down and talk about this, including what to do about the deposits. We can e-mail our kids to get their reactions. I'd like to see a list of pros and cons and what is important to us for a vacation.

19. **Interviewer:** That's okay with me.

20. **Interviewee:** What about the news reports about cruise ships coming back early with hundreds of people ill from mysterious ailments? That's all we need is to have everyone get sick.

21. **Interviewer:** Well, that happens occasionally, but news reports exaggerate the problem. None of the people have more serious problems than flu-like symptoms.

22. **Interviewee:** And *you* need to do some serious research into cruises, including availability, costs, activities, island stops, causes and frequencies of illness, and such. Think about the young children and what they will do. How safe it is? Will we all get seasick?

23. **Interviewer:** I can do that. In fact, I stopped by King Travel a couple of days ago and picked up several brochures. Kyle and Peggy will bring me some of the literature they have saved from their trips. They tell me seasickness can be avoided with ginger candy.

24. **Interviewee:** I'm really skeptical about changing our plans at this late date, but maybe we could consider it in a few years. I love the beach and being able to take long walks in the surf in the mornings and evenings.

25. **Interviewer:** You wouldn't be giving up the beach because most cruise ships stop at islands with beautiful beaches. Take a look at this one on St. Thomas. Here's another one from St. Croix.

26. **Interviewee:** They are beautiful, but I wonder how you get there from the ship. Let me see what Jim thinks about it. We can talk at dinner tonight. You realize what a golf nut he is and how much he loves the courses in the Myrtle Beach area.

27. **Interviewer:** Actually, I haven't mentioned it to Jack yet. I wanted to get your reactions first.

28. **Interviewee:** I'm willing to talk and think about it, but I'm about 98% opposed to changing this year. You're got a big sales job to do, and not just on me but the other members of our two families. They're excited about the new condos and eating at Sharkeys. That's become a tradition in our family.

29. **Interviewer:** I know that. It's been fun for several years, but I feel if I can get you on my side, we may be on a cruise before you know it.

30. **Interviewee:** Don't count on it.

31. **Interviewer:** I'm not, but I'm ready to do my homework for the next time we meet. How about Saturday morning after the soccer game.

32. **Interviewee:** Okay. I'll see what Jim thinks. We usually talk to the kids on the phone over the weekend, and I will sound them out.

33. **Interviewer:** Okay. See you on Saturday. I think a cruise would be a great adventure, something none of us has ever done.

34. **Interviewee:** It might be more adventure than we can handle.

Critical Thinking Exercise

Identify the following as reasoning from: (a) accepted belief, (b) condition, (c) two choices, (d) example, (e) facts, (f) comparison or analogy, or (g) cause-effect.

1. _____ This insurance policy is like an umbrella. It will protect you from all sorts of rainy days: storm damage to your condo, fire and water damage to your furnishings, accidents to you and friends who might be visiting, and theft of anything in the condo, storage, or garage, including your car.

2. _____ Studies by the American Medical Association show that regular exercise at least three times a week will add ten years to our lives. Exercise obviously will add years to your life.

3. _____ You have two ways to finance your graduate work in occupational therapy: low-interest government-backed loans or scholarships. Scholarships are extremely rare for this area, so a low-interest loan is your best bet.

4. _____ If you take a small dose, 81 mg aspirin once a day, you are less likely to have a heart attack. You should start taking one each day.

5. _____ When police arrived at her apartment, they found all of the doors and windows locked. There was no evidence of forced entry. They could find no evidence that she had been attacked in any way. It's obvious that she died of natural causes.

6. _____ Either you start on this project now, or you are not going to get it finished by the deadline. I see no evidence that you are planning to start, so you are going to miss your deadline.

7. _____ Everyone knows that health care costs are out of control and that we must find less expensive testing procedures. This procedure you are developing is going to be at least 25% more expensive than the current procedure. It's obvious that your procedure is not going to be adopted.

8. _____ In a study of 650 students who used the Writing Lab to work on research papers, over 85% received grades of A or B. Using the Writing Lab will lead to better grades on your written projects.

9. _____ This ski facility is very much like the one you visited in Idaho last year. It has several runs that require differing skills, it always has adequate natural snowfall, and the lodge has rooms in the same price range. It also has bus and air service each day. I think you will like it.

10. _____ This was a very sound investment until the severe recession of 2008–2010 that caused problems for nearly all investments. We're not likely to see one of those recessions in our lifetime, so it's a good time to put your money in this investment.

Identification of Persuasive Tactics Exercise

Interview parties use a variety of persuasive tactics to change the other's way of thinking, feeling, and/or acting. Identify the persuasive tactic used in each of the following statements as bifurcation, *post hoc* or scrambling cause-effect, hasty generalization, comparison, thin entering wedge, overt identification, identification through association, identification through disassociation, bandwagon, *ad hominem,* guilt by association, or transfer of guilt.

1. I'm a college student like you, so I would not be recommending this study abroad program if it would delay your graduation.

2. Global warming is a hoax. Just look at how cold this winter has been with record snowfalls in parts of the South that never get snow.

3. This is an excellent health care plan just like the one members of Congress enjoy. Like theirs, it is affordable, comprehensive, cannot be denied because of pre-existing conditions, and cannot be cancelled if you develop a catastrophic medical condition.

4. Look, you have only two choices when selecting a full-size pickup: Chevy or Ford. Ford has the highest ratings by owners, so you should buy a Ford.

5. I got the flu right after I got that flu shot. It's obvious that the shot gave me the flu.

6. Everybody I've talked to is going to spend spring break in Mexico. You ought to come with us too.

7. Our Tea Party movement is not part of any political party. We're independent-minded people who are fed up with taxes, big government, the ever-expanding national debt, and the constant erosion of our fundamental rights. Anybody with these concerns can join; not just Republicans.

8. Can you believe what those idiots in the financial aid office just decided about registering late for classes? It's obvious that they didn't have to work or borrow to get a good education.

9. I studied over eight hours for this exam and still got a C–. Professor Smarts can't write clear questions or grade what we actually write. I think he just skims over our answers and does not take into account what we really know.

10. If we let workers give input into the hiring process, they will soon want to have a say in scheduling, production, promotion, and termination decisions.

Tests of Evidence Exercise

The persuader in the "An Organic Farming Operation" case is attempting to convince a neighbor to start an organic farming operation on 100 acres of his farm by using the following pieces of evidence. Judge the strength of *each piece* of evidence and the evidence *as a whole* by asking the following questions:

- ☐ Is the source of evidence unbiased and reliable?
- ☐ Is the source authoritative in this field?
- ☐ Is the evidence documented by source, date, and location?
- ☐ Is the evidence the most recent available?
- ☐ Is the evidence communicated accurately and in context?
- ☐ Is the evidence sufficient in quantity?
- ☐ Is the evidence sufficient in quality?

1. In a recent newspaper piece, Governor McBride stated that organic farming in our state has been growing at some 24% each year and produces the safest produce on the market.

2. Last summer I conducted a survey of those attending farmer's markets in 13 locations around the mid-South. They said they purchased only organically grown fruits and vegetables and had seen changes in the health of their families.

3. Abigail Ewing, editor of *The Organic Farmer*, reported in the April 2007 issue that organic farmers were able to ask 15–20% higher prices for their produce because consumers were turning in large numbers to organically grown produce because they saw it as healthier and less of a danger to their health and that of their children. There is a growing concern for the chemicals used in traditional agriculture.

4. Organic farming is much like the farming used by our ancestors before we began to use a variety of chemicals in large quantities to allegedly improve the quality of the food we eat. Many health problems, particularly allergies in children, were virtually unknown prior to World War II and the development of herbicides and pesticides.

5. You know Jake Chin who farms near Chesterfield? He told me that his expenditures have dropped 37% and his income has risen by 18% since he began a no-till, organic farming operation six years ago. I know Jake's experience is common among organic farmers.

chapter five

Performance Review Interviewing

Performance Review Interview Assignment

The purpose of this assignment is to provide you with realistic and somewhat difficult experiences in conducting and taking part in performance review interviews. We will provide you with adequate opportunities to make this assignment as realistic and relevant as possible.

Instructions for Interviewers

1. You have three options when selecting a case for this assignment: (a) select a performance case from your textbook, (b) modify one of the textbook cases, or (c) create a case of your own. If you modify or create a case, please submit a draft of this case to your instructor for approval by _____. Option b and c cases must be of the same level of difficulty as the ones in your textbook.

2. Structure a performance review interview according to one of the performance models introduced in your textbook. Be sure to adapt to the interviewee and the situation. You will need more than a simple question schedule for this assignment.

3. Use the real names and genders of the interview parties; not ones that might be provided in the printed cases.

4. Involve your interviewee actively in the interview.

5. Create realistic evidence and documentation to support your performance review.

6. Each interview will be _____ minutes long.

7. Your interview will be worth a possible _____ points.

Instructions for Interviewees

1. Study your case and role thoroughly.

2. Take an active part in the interview.

3. Insist that the performance review model be followed.

4. Provide input into your performance.

5. Challenge the interviewer's evaluations, evidence, and documentation when necessary.

6. Work out agreements and sign off on them.

7. Your role in the interview will be worth a possible _____ points.

Performance Interview Critique: Interviewer Form A

Interviewer _____ Critic _____

Opening . . . . 1 2 3 4 5 × _____ = _____

Coaching approach . . . . 1 2 3 4 5 × _____ = _____

Coverage of total performance . . . . 1 2 3 4 5 × _____ = _____

Avoidance of common biases . . . . 1 2 3 4 5 × _____ = _____

Use of questions . . . . 1 2 3 4 5 × _____ = _____

New goals . . . . 1 2 3 4 5 × _____ = _____

Involves the interviewee . . . . 1 2 3 4 5 × _____ = _____

Communication skills . . . . 1 2 3 4 5 × _____ = _____

Total Points _____

Comments:

Grading Scale:
   1 poor
   2 below average
   3 average
   4 above average
   5 excellent

Performance Interview Critique: Interviewer Form A

Interviewer _____ Critic _____

Opening 1   2   3   4   5   × _____ = _____

Coaching approach 1   2   3   4   5   × _____ = _____

Coverage of total performance 1   2   3   4   5   × _____ = _____

Avoidance of common biases 1   2   3   4   5   × _____ = _____

Use of questions 1   2   3   4   5   × _____ = _____

New goals 1   2   3   4   5   × _____ = _____

Involves the interviewee 1   2   3   4   5   × _____ = _____

Communication skills 1   2   3   4   5   × _____ = _____

Total Points _____

Comments:

Grading Scale:
   1 poor
   2 below average
   3 average
   4 above average
   5 excellent

Performance Interview Critique: Interviewer Form A

Interviewer _____ Critic _____

Opening . . . . 1 2 3 4 5 × _____ = _____

Coaching approach . . . . 1 2 3 4 5 × _____ = _____

Coverage of total performance . . . . 1 2 3 4 5 × _____ = _____

Avoidance of common biases . . . . 1 2 3 4 5 × _____ = _____

Use of questions . . . . 1 2 3 4 5 × _____ = _____

New goals . . . . 1 2 3 4 5 × _____ = _____

Involves the interviewee . . . . 1 2 3 4 5 × _____ = _____

Communication skills . . . . 1 2 3 4 5 × _____ = _____

Total Points _____

Comments:

Grading Scale:
  1 poor
  2 below average
  3 average
  4 above average
  5 excellent

Performance Interview Critique: Interviewer Form B

Interviewer _____ Critic _____

_____

Opening: greeting, rapport, orientation

_____ Points _____

Coaching approach: two-way communication, feedback, positive reinforcement

_____ Points _____

Coverage of total performance: standards that are met, positive integration of work and results, needed improvements, handling of controversies, factual, performance-related information, input from the interviewee

_____ Points _____

Avoidance of common biases: gender bias, halo effect, pitchfork effect, central tendency, recency error, length of service, loose/tight/competitive rating

_____ Points _____

Use of questions: open-ended, neutral, probing

_____ Points _____

New goals: appropriate number, specific and well-defined, appropriate degree of difficulty, input from the interviewee, agreement with interviewee

_____ Points _____

Involvement of the interviewee

_____ Points _____

Communication skills: verbal, nonverbal, listening

_____ Points _____

Total Points _____

Performance Interview Critique: Interviewer Form B

Interviewer _____ Critic _____

Opening: greeting, rapport, orientation

Points _____

Coaching approach: two-way communication, feedback, positive reinforcement

Points _____

Coverage of total performance: standards that are met, positive integration of work and results, needed improvements, handling of controversies, factual, performance-related information, input from the interviewee

Points _____

Avoidance of common biases: gender bias, halo effect, pitchfork effect, central tendency, recency error, length of service, loose/tight/competitive rating

Points _____

Use of questions: open-ended, neutral, probing

Points _____

New goals: appropriate number, specific and well-defined, appropriate degree of difficulty, input from the interviewee, agreement with interviewee

Points _____

Involvement of the interviewee

Points _____

Communication skills: verbal, nonverbal, listening

Points _____

Total Points _____

Performance Interview Critique: Interviewer Form B

Interviewer _____ Critic _____

Opening: greeting, rapport, orientation

Points _____

Coaching approach: two-way communication, feedback, positive reinforcement

Points _____

Coverage of total performance: standards that are met, positive integration of work and results, needed improvements, handling of controversies, factual, performance-related information, input from the interviewee

Points _____

Avoidance of common biases: gender bias, halo effect, pitchfork effect, central tendency, recency error, length of service, loose/tight/competitive rating

Points _____

Use of questions: open-ended, neutral, probing

Points _____

New goals: appropriate number, specific and well-defined, appropriate degree of difficulty, input from the interviewee, agreement with interviewee

Points _____

Involvement of the interviewee

Points _____

Communication skills: verbal, nonverbal, listening

Points _____

Total Points _____

Performance Interview Critique: Interviewee Form A

Interviewee _____ Critic _____

Evidence of preparation . . . . 1 2 3 4 5 ✕ _____ = _____

Answers to questions . . . . 1 2 3 4 5 ✕ _____ = _____

Handling of problems . . . . 1 2 3 4 5 ✕ _____ = _____

Information gathering . . . . 1 2 3 4 5 ✕ _____ = _____

Questions . . . . 1 2 3 4 5 ✕ _____ = _____

Setting of priorities . . . . 1 2 3 4 5 ✕ _____ = _____

Plays an active role in the interview . . . . 1 2 3 4 5 ✕ _____ = _____

Communication skills . . . . 1 2 3 4 5 ✕ _____ = _____

Total Points _____

Comments:

Grading Scale:
1 poor
2 below average
3 average
4 above average
5 excellent

Performance Interview Critique: Interviewee Form A

Interviewee _____ Critic _____

Evidence of preparation . . . . 1 2 3 4 5 × _____ = _____

Answers to questions . . . . 1 2 3 4 5 × _____ = _____

Handling of problems . . . . 1 2 3 4 5 × _____ = _____

Information gathering . . . . 1 2 3 4 5 × _____ = _____

Questions . . . . 1 2 3 4 5 × _____ = _____

Setting of priorities . . . . 1 2 3 4 5 × _____ = _____

Plays an active role in the interview . . . . 1 2 3 4 5 × _____ = _____

Communication skills . . . . 1 2 3 4 5 × _____ = _____

Total Points _____

Comments:

Grading Scale:
1 poor
2 below average
3 average
4 above average
5 excellent

Performance Interview Critique: Interviewee Form A

Interviewee _____ Critic _____

Evidence of preparation 1   2   3   4   5   × _____ = _____

Answers to questions 1   2   3   4   5   × _____ = _____

Handling of problems 1   2   3   4   5   × _____ = _____

Information gathering 1   2   3   4   5   × _____ = _____

Questions 1   2   3   4   5   × _____ = _____

Setting of priorities 1   2   3   4   5   × _____ = _____

Plays an active role in the interview 1   2   3   4   5   × _____ = _____

Communication skills 1   2   3   4   5   × _____ = _____

Total Points _____

Comments:

Grading Scale:
1 poor
2 below average
3 average
4 above average
5 excellent

Performance Interview Critique: Interviewee Form B

Interviewee _____ Critic _____

_____

Evidence of preparation: objectives reached, standards of measure, problem areas, ways to improve

Points _____

_____

Answers to questions: thorough, honest, to the point, emphasis on strengths and accomplishments, clarification of questions

Points _____

_____

Handling of problems: explanations and not excuses, acceptance of criticism, seeking suggestion

Points _____

_____

Information gathering: prospects for advancement, feedback on performance, expectations of interviewer

Points _____

_____

Questions: open-ended, avoids common question pitfalls, performance-oriented, not defensive

Points _____

_____

Setting of priorities: short-range, long-range, realistic

Points _____

_____

Plays an active role in the interview

Points _____

_____

Communication skills: verbal, nonverbal, listening

Points _____

_____

Total Points _____

Performance Interview Critique: Interviewee Form B

Interviewee _____ Critic _____

_____

Evidence of preparation: objectives reached, standards of measure, problem areas, ways to improve

Points _____
_____

Answers to questions: thorough, honest, to the point, emphasis on strengths and accomplishments, clarification of questions

Points _____
_____

Handling of problems: explanations and not excuses, acceptance of criticism, seeking suggestion

Points _____
_____

Information gathering: prospects for advancement, feedback on performance, expectations of interviewer

Points _____
_____

Questions: open-ended, avoids common question pitfalls, performance-oriented, not defensive

Points _____
_____

Setting of priorities: short-range, long-range, realistic

Points _____
_____

Plays an active role in the interview

Points _____
_____

Communication skills: verbal, nonverbal, listening

Points _____
_____

Total Points _____

Performance Interview Critique: Interviewee Form B

Interviewee _____ Critic _____

_____

Evidence of preparation: objectives reached, standards of measure, problem areas, ways to improve

Points _____

Answers to questions: thorough, honest, to the point, emphasis on strengths and accomplishments, clarification of questions

Points _____

Handling of problems: explanations and not excuses, acceptance of criticism, seeking suggestion

Points _____

Information gathering: prospects for advancement, feedback on performance, expectations of interviewer

Points _____

Questions: open-ended, avoids common question pitfalls, performance-oriented, not defensive

Points _____

Setting of priorities: short-range, long-range, realistic

Points _____

Plays an active role in the interview

Points _____

Communication skills: verbal, nonverbal, listening

Points _____

Total Points _____

chapter
SIX

Counseling Interviewing

Counseling Interview Assignment

The purpose of this assignment is to provide you with a realistic and somewhat difficult experience in conducting a counseling interview. We will provide you with adequate opportunities to make this assignment as realistic and relevant as possible.

Instructions for Interviewers

1. You have three options when selecting a case for this assignment: (a) select a counseling case from your textbook, (b) modify one of the textbook cases, or (c) create a counseling case of your own. If you modify or create a case, please submit a draft of this case to your instructor for approval by _____. Option b and c cases must be of the same level of difficulty as the ones in your textbook.

2. Develop an interviewing approach (directive or nondirective) or combination of approaches appropriate for the case selected, modified, or developed.

3. Use the real names and genders of the interview parties; not ones that might be provided in printed cases.

4. If appropriate, create a counseling report form that contains realistic data.

5. Involve your interviewee actively in the interview.

6.   Each interview will be _____ minutes long.

7.   Your interview will be worth a possible _____ points.

Instructions for Interviewees

1.   Study your case and role thoroughly.

2.   Take an active part in the interview.

3.   Challenge the interviewer's comments, questions, evaluations, and recommendations.

Counseling Interview Critique: Counselor Form A

Counselor _____   Critic _____

Opening 1   2   3   4   5   × _____ = _____

Appropriate approach(es) 1   2   3   4   5   × _____ = _____

Listening and observing. 1   2   3   4   5   × _____ = _____

Use of questions 1   2   3   4   5   × _____ = _____

Encourages input 1   2   3   4   5   × _____ = _____

Responses to questions 1   2   3   4   5   × _____ = _____

Closing 1   2   3   4   5   × _____ = _____

Supportive climate 1   2   3   4   5   × _____ = _____

Communication skills 1   2   3   4   5   × _____ = _____

Total Points _____

Comments:

Grading Scale:

1 poor
2 below average
3 average
4 above average
5 excellent

Counseling Interview Critique: Counselor Form A

Counselor _____ Critic _____

Opening . . . . 1 2 3 4 5 × _____ = _____

Appropriate approach(es) . . . . 1 2 3 4 5 × _____ = _____

Listening and observing . . . . 1 2 3 4 5 × _____ = _____

Use of questions . . . . 1 2 3 4 5 × _____ = _____

Encourages input . . . . 1 2 3 4 5 × _____ = _____

Responses to questions . . . . 1 2 3 4 5 × _____ = _____

Closing . . . . 1 2 3 4 5 × _____ = _____

Supportive climate . . . . 1 2 3 4 5 × _____ = _____

Communication skills . . . . 1 2 3 4 5 × _____ = _____

Total Points _____

Comments:

Grading Scale:
1 poor
2 below average
3 average
4 above average
5 excellent

Counseling Interview Critique: Counselor Form A

Counselor _____ Critic _____

Opening . . . . 1 2 3 4 5 × _____ = _____

Appropriate approach(es) . . . . 1 2 3 4 5 × _____ = _____

Listening and observing . . . . 1 2 3 4 5 × _____ = _____

Use of questions . . . . 1 2 3 4 5 × _____ = _____

Encourages input . . . . 1 2 3 4 5 × _____ = _____

Responses to questions . . . . 1 2 3 4 5 × _____ = _____

Closing . . . . 1 2 3 4 5 × _____ = _____

Supportive climate . . . . 1 2 3 4 5 × _____ = _____

Communication skills . . . . 1 2 3 4 5 × _____ = _____

Total Points _____

Comments:

Grading Scale:
   1 poor
   2 below average
   3 average
   4 above average
   5 excellent

Counseling Interview Critique: Counselor Form B

Counselor _____ Critic _____

_____

Opening: greeting, setting appropriate tone, rapport, orientation

Points _____

_____

Appropriate approach(es): directive, nondirective, combination

Points _____

_____

Listening/observing: for comprehension, empathy, evaluation, resolution

Points _____

_____

Use of questions: open-ended, probing, avoidance of pitfalls

Points _____

_____

Encourages input

Points _____

_____

Responses to questions: highly nondirective, nondirective, directive, highly directive

Points _____

_____

Closing: techniques, no new topics, sincere and honest, agreement on course of action

Points _____

_____

Supportive climate: quiet and private location, free of interruptions, appropriate seating

Points _____

_____

Communication skills: verbal, nonverbal

Points _____

_____

Total Points _____

Counseling Interview Critique: Counselor Form B

Counselor _____ Critic _____

Opening: greeting, setting appropriate tone, rapport, orientation

Points _____

Appropriate approach(es): directive, nondirective, combination

Points _____

Listening/observing: for comprehension, empathy, evaluation, resolution

Points _____

Use of questions: open-ended, probing, avoidance of pitfalls

Points _____

Encourages input

Points _____

Responses to questions: highly nondirective, nondirective, directive, highly directive

Points _____

Closing: techniques, no new topics, sincere and honest, agreement on course of action

Points _____

Supportive climate: quiet and private location, free of interruptions, appropriate seating

Points _____

Communication skills: verbal, nonverbal

Points _____

Total Points _____

Counseling Interview Critique: Counselor Form B

Counselor _____   Critic _____

_____

Opening: greeting, setting appropriate tone, rapport, orientation

Points _____

Appropriate approach(es): directive, nondirective, combination

Points _____

Listening/observing: for comprehension, empathy, evaluation, resolution

Points _____

Use of questions: open-ended, probing, avoidance of pitfalls

Points _____

Encourages input

Points _____

Responses to questions: highly nondirective, nondirective, directive, highly directive

Points _____

Closing: techniques, no new topics, sincere and honest, agreement on course of action

Points _____

Supportive climate: quiet and private location, free of interruptions, appropriate seating

Points _____

Communication skills: verbal, nonverbal

Points _____

Total Points _____

chapter **seven**

Health Care Interviewing

The purpose of this assignment is to provide you with a realistic and somewhat difficult experience in conducting a health care interview. We will provide you with adequate opportunities to make this assignment as realistic and relevant as possible.

Instructions for Interviewers

1. You have three options when selecting a case for this assignment: (a) select a health care case from your textbook, (b) modify one of the textbook cases, or (c) create a health care case of your own. If you modify or create a case, please submit a draft of this case to your instructor for approval by _____.

2. Develop an interviewing approach (directive or nondirective) or combination of approaches appropriate for the case selected, modified, or created.

3. Use the real names and genders of the interview parties; not ones that might be provided in printed cases.

4. Involve your interviewee actively in the interview.

5. Each interview will be _____ minutes long.

6. Your interview will be worth a possible _____ points.

Instructions for Interviewees

1. Study your case and role thoroughly.

2. Take an active part in the interview.

3. Challenge the interviewer's comments, questions, evaluations, and recommendations.

Health Care Interview Critique: Interviewer Form A

Interviewer _____ Critic _____

Opening . . . . 1 2 3 4 5 × _____ = _____

Enhances the relationship . . . . 1 2 3 4 5 × _____ = _____

Fosters collaboration . . . . 1 2 3 4 5 × _____ = _____

Information getting. . . . . 1 2 3 4 5 × _____ = _____

Information giving . . . . 1 2 3 4 5 × _____ = _____

Counseling and persuading. . . . . 1 2 3 4 5 × _____ = _____

Appropriate approach(es) . . . . 1 2 3 4 5 × _____ = _____

Listening. . . . . 1 2 3 4 5 × _____ = _____

Communication skills . . . . 1 2 3 4 5 × _____ = _____

Closing . . . . 1 2 3 4 5 × _____ = _____

Total Points _____

Comments:

Grading Scale:

    1 poor
    2 below average
    3 average
    4 above average

Health Care Interview Critique: Interviewer Form A

Interviewer _____ Critic _____

Opening . . . . 1 2 3 4 5 × _____ = _____

Enhances the relationship . . . . 1 2 3 4 5 × _____ = _____

Fosters collaboration . . . . 1 2 3 4 5 × _____ = _____

Information getting. . . . . 1 2 3 4 5 × _____ = _____

Information giving . . . . 1 2 3 4 5 × _____ = _____

Counseling and persuading. . . . . 1 2 3 4 5 × _____ = _____

Appropriate approach(es) . . . . 1 2 3 4 5 × _____ = _____

Listening. . . . . 1 2 3 4 5 × _____ = _____

Communication skills . . . . 1 2 3 4 5 × _____ = _____

Closing . . . . 1 2 3 4 5 × _____ = _____

Total Points _____

Comments:

Grading Scale:

   1 poor

   2 below average

   3 average

   4 above average

Health Care Interview Critique: Interviewer Form A

Interviewer _____ Critic _____

Opening . . . . 1 2 3 4 5 × _____ = _____

Enhances the relationship . . . . 1 2 3 4 5 × _____ = _____

Fosters collaboration . . . . 1 2 3 4 5 × _____ = _____

Information getting. . . . . 1 2 3 4 5 × _____ = _____

Information giving . . . . 1 2 3 4 5 × _____ = _____

Counseling and persuading. . . . . 1 2 3 4 5 × _____ = _____

Appropriate approach(es) . . . . 1 2 3 4 5 × _____ = _____

Listening. . . . . 1 2 3 4 5 × _____ = _____

Communication skills . . . . 1 2 3 4 5 × _____ = _____

Closing . . . . 1 2 3 4 5 × _____ = _____

Total Points _____

Comments:

Grading Scale:

    1 poor
    2 below average
    3 average
    4 above average
    5 excellent

Health Care Interview Critique: Interviewer Form B

Interviewer _____ Critic _____

_____

Opening: greeting, rapport, orientation

Points _____

Enhances relationship: relaxed and confident, shows interest, maintains objectivity, sincere and honest, appropriate control

Points _____

Fosters collaboration: co-agents in a problem-solving context

Points _____

Information getting: funnel sequence, open questions, probing into questions, detection of clues, avoids question pitfalls

Points _____

Information giving: trust and confidence, avoids information overload, variety of media, defines and translates terms, clear organization

Points _____

Counseling and persuading: appropriate climate, encourages interaction, range of responses and reactions, considering solutions

Points _____

Appropriate approach(es): nondirective, directive, combination

Points _____

Listening: comprehension, empathy, evaluation, resolution

Points _____

Communication skills: verbal, nonverbal

Points _____

Closing: techniques, sincere, honest

Points _____

Total Points _____

Health Care Interview Critique: Interviewer Form B

Interviewer _____ Critic _____

Opening: greeting, rapport, orientation

Points _____

Enhances relationship: relaxed and confident, shows interest, maintains objectivity, sincere and honest, appropriate control

Points _____

Fosters collaboration: co-agents in a problem-solving context

Points _____

Information getting: funnel sequence, open questions, probing into questions, detection of clues, avoids question pitfalls

Points _____

Information giving: trust and confidence, avoids information overload, variety of media, defines and translates terms, clear organization

Points _____

Counseling and persuading: appropriate climate, encourages interaction, range of responses and reactions, considering solutions

Points _____

Appropriate approach(es): nondirective, directive, combination

Points _____

Listening: comprehension, empathy, evaluation, resolution

Points _____

Communication skills: verbal, nonverbal

Points _____

Closing: techniques, sincere, honest

Points _____

Total Points _____

Health Care Interview Critique: Interviewer Form B

Interviewer _____ Critic _____

Opening: greeting, rapport, orientation

Points _____

Enhances relationship: relaxed and confident, shows interest, maintains objectivity, sincere and honest, appropriate control

Points _____

Fosters collaboration: co-agents in a problem-solving context

Points _____

Information getting: funnel sequence, open questions, probing into questions, detection of clues, avoids question pitfalls

Points _____

Information giving: trust and confidence, avoids information overload, variety of media, defines and translates terms, clear organization

Points _____

Counseling and persuading: appropriate climate, encourages interaction, range of responses and reactions, considering solutions

Points _____

Appropriate approach(es): nondirective, directive, combination

Points _____

Listening: comprehension, empathy, evaluation, resolution

Points _____

Communication skills: verbal, nonverbal

Points _____

Closing: techniques, sincere, honest

Points _____

Total Points _____

chapter
eight

Field Interview Project

Field Project Assignment

Students in interviewing courses have unlimited opportunities for real-life interview projects outside of the classroom. Faculty, administrators, students, neighbors, managers, personnel directors, counselors, journalists, editors, recruiters, sales representatives, police officers, attorneys, and others serve willingly as interviewees. They like to see students taking textbook and classroom learning into the field. Outside projects can also help students learn how to conduct research or to make career decisions by interviewing persons in their fields of study.

This field project assignment is designed to give you an opportunity to conduct one or more *real-life*, non-role-playing interviews outside of the classroom setting. The *worth of this assignment* to you and your training in interviewing *depends entirely on you* because you will pick an option, select a topic, develop an appropriate schedule of questions, select interviewees, and conduct the interviews. It will be a waste of time only if *you* decide not to take this assignment seriously. It can be the most valuable experience of the course and perhaps of your college career. Field projects often lead to internships, summer positions, job interviews, and positions upon graduation.

This assignment will proceed through five stages. Each stage is critical to the value and success of your field project.

Stage 1: Select a project option, topic, and do necessary background research and reading.

1. Select from one of three types of field projects that will provide the most valuable experiences and information for you.

    a. A single in-depth interview lasting approximately __2__ minutes/(hours.) This option is best when a subject with unique expertise or experiences is willing to submit to a lengthy, in-depth interview. Note: You may divide this interaction into two or more interviews if the interviewee has neither the time nor energy for one lengthy interview.

        Topics Related To:
        • Career related
        • Problem solving
        • Class
        • Personal interest
        • Family History

        e.g., The interview training and experiences of a college recruiter.

        The interviewing techniques of a sports broadcaster.

        A typical day in the life of a sales representative.

        The experiences of a veteran of the D-Day invasion.

    b. Two or more interviews with a minimum length of __60__ minutes each. This option is best when you want two or more opinions, reactions, or accounts.

        e.g., The future of managed health care.

        What recruiters look for in college graduates.

        The experiences of journalists covering fatal accidents.

    c. A series of "experimental" interviews in which one or more variables are manipulated with a minimum length of __60__ minutes each. This option will allow you to see how different interview variables affect the outcome of two series of interviews.

        e.g., Leading versus neutral questions.

        The influence of interviewer appearance on interviewee responses.

        Information from open and closed questions.

2. Select a topic of interest and value to you. It may or may not be interview related. Perhaps it will help you make an important career decision or learn more about a family member.

3. Do necessary background research and reading. This project provides you with an opportunity to study interview types that we will not address at length in class: employee performance problems, counseling, performance review, and health care.

Stage 2: Prepare a two page project proposal. It is due by __9/16__ and is worth a possible _____ points.

1. Explain which option you have selected and what your general topic will be. How will your interview time of __2 hours__ ~~minutes~~ be divided?

2. Explain your motivation for selecting this option and how you hope to use the information gathered. For instance, is it for discovering interview methods or effects, self-enrichment, research for another class, learning about future career options, or determining a future course of action?

3. Who do you plan to interview? How many people do you plan to interview? If you cannot name names at this time, list characteristics of ideal interviewees: small business owner, sales representative, academic counselor, basketball coach, police officer, researcher, recruiter, broadcast journalist, survivor of a prisoner of war camp.

4. When and where do you plan to conduct your interview(s)?

5. Describe any problems that might arise with this project such as time, distance, and availability of interviewees.

Stage 3: Prepare an interview guide. It is due by _____9/26_____ **and is worth** _____ **points.**

1. Provide a brief introductory paragraph that explains which structural sequence(s) you selected and why.

2. Develop your guide in outline format.

3. Your guide needs to be as lengthy as necessary to accomplish the interview task you have set for yourself. For example, a single in-depth interview will require a much longer guide than a series of 15–20 minute interviews.

Stage 4: Conduct one or more interviews.

1. The length of each interview depends upon the assignment option you have selected.

2. Do not interview two or more people simultaneously (roommates, husband and wife, two police officers) because the answers of one are likely to affect the other's answers.

3. Strangers or mere acquaintances may be more difficult to approach, but they tend to be easier to interview than friends and relatives who feel free to give you a tough time and wander off the topic, perhaps demanding to know how you would answer your own questions.

4. If you deviate from your prepared question schedule, be sure to write these questions down during your interviews so they can be reported in Stage 5. It will be of value to both you and your instructor to see the nature of these questions and the purposes they served. p. (257-265)

5. Leave with each interviewee a copy of the **Field Interview Critique Form** and a stamped envelope addressed to your instructor. These critiques will not be read until after your project is graded, and then they will be attached to your project to give you feedback on how well you conducted your interview(s). Your instructor's address is:

   Brian Lamb School of Communications, Rm 214

   Beering Hall

   Check BLK Board

6. Send a thank you note.

Stage 5: Prepare a written post-interview report. It is due by _____10/28_____ **and is worth a possible** _____ **points.**

1. Provide a copy of your final schedule of questions, including unplanned questions placed within brackets [ ]. Indicate which of your original questions you did not ask and why.

2. Write an analysis of your interview(s) that addresses the following questions:

   a. Who did you interview and why?

   b. Which opening techniques did you use and why?

   c. Which closing techniques did you use and why?

   d. How did you record information received and why?

   Describe the communication that occurred between you and your interviewee(s).

f.   What, if any, unforeseen problems developed? How did you deal with them?

g.   How did location(s) affect your interviews?

h.   What three things did you learn about interviewing principles and practices?

i.   If you were doing this field project over again, what would you do differently?

3.   Write a ~~two-page~~ *1 page* summary of the information you received from your interview(s).

4.   Attach a **Record for Field Project Interviews** from your project text.

5.   This report should be 6–7 pages in length *excluding* your schedule of questions and the **Record for Field Project Interviews**.

Stage 2: Field Project Proposal Critique

Name _____

Option selected and why . . . . 1 2 3 4 5 × _____ = _____

Topic selected and why. . . . . 1 2 3 4 5 × _____ = _____

Motive for selecting this option and topic . . . . 1 2 3 4 5 × _____ = _____

Who will be interviewed and why . . . . 1 2 3 4 5 × _____ = _____

When and where will the interviews
take place . . . . 1 2 3 4 5 × _____ = _____

Potential problems for this project . . . . 1 2 3 4 5 × _____ = _____

Total Points _____

Suggestions:

Grading Scale:
1 poor
2 below average
3 average
4 above average

Stage 3: Field Project Interview Guide

Name _____

Introductory paragraph   1   2   3   4   5   ✕ _____ = _____

Explanation of structural sequence   1   2   3   4   5   ✕ _____ = _____

Guide in standard outline format   1   2   3   4   5   ✕ _____ = _____

Sub- or probing areas included   1   2   3   4   5   ✕ _____ = _____

Proper length for each interview   1   2   3   4   5   ✕ _____ = _____

Total Points _____

Suggestions:

Grading Scale:
  1 poor
  2 below average
  3 average
  4 above average

Stage 5: Field Project Post-Interview Report

Name _____

Final schedule of questions

    Planned primary and probing questions . . . . 1 2 3 4 5 × _____ = _____

    Unplanned primary and probing questions . . . . 1 2 3 4 5 × _____ = _____

    Original questions not asked and why . . . . 1 2 3 4 5 × _____ = _____

Analysis of your interviews

    Who did you interview and why? . . . . 1 2 3 4 5 × _____ = _____

    Which opening techniques were used and why? . . . 1 2 3 4 5 × _____ = _____

    Which closing techniques were used and why? . . . . 1 2 3 4 5 × _____ = _____

    How was information recorded and why? . . . . 1 2 3 4 5 × _____ = _____

    How would you describe the interviews? . . . . 1 2 3 4 5 × _____ = _____

    How did you handle unforeseen problems? . . . . 1 2 3 4 5 × _____ = _____

    How did location(s) affect your interviews? . . . . 1 2 3 4 5 × _____ = _____

    What three things did you learn about
    interviewing? . . . . 1 2 3 4 5 × _____ = _____

    What would you do differently? . . . . 1 2 3 4 5 × _____ = _____

Two-page summary of the information received . . . . 1 2 3 4 5 × _____ = _____

Attached **Record for Field Project Interviews** . . . . 1 2 3 4 5 × _____ = _____

Total Points _____

Comments:

Grading Scale:
    1 poor
    2 below average
    3 average
    4 above average

Field Interview Critique Form

Student's Name _____   Instructor's Name _____

Please complete this form and return it as soon as possible. Your comments will be of greater value to the student if they are stated frankly and specifically. This report will have no bearing on the student's grade. Its sole purpose is to provide the student with an objective review from a person outside of the classroom.

1. How effectively did the student initiate the interview and establish rapport with you?

2. How effective was the structure of the interview?

3. How effective were the student's questioning skills?

4. How effective were the student's communication skills: language, nonverbal communication, listening?

5. How effectively did the student close the interview?

6. What specific suggestions would you offer this student to improve his/her interviewing skills?

Interviewee's Signature _____

Interviewee's Address _____

Date of the Interview _____   Length of the Interview _____

Field Interview Critique Form

Student's Name _____ Instructor's Name _____

Please complete this form and return it as soon as possible. Your comments will be of greater value to the student if they are stated frankly and specifically. This report will have no bearing on the student's grade. Its sole purpose is to provide the student with an objective review from a person outside of the classroom.

1. How effectively did the student initiate the interview and establish rapport with you?

2. How effective was the structure of the interview?

3. How effective were the student's questioning skills?

4. How effective were the student's communication skills: language, nonverbal communication, listening?

5. How effectively did the student close the interview?

6. What specific suggestions would you offer this student to improve his/her interviewing skills?

Interviewee's Signature _____

Interviewee's Address _____

Date of the Interview _____ Length of the Interview _____

Field Interview Critique Form

Student's Name _____ Instructor's Name _____

Please complete this form and return it as soon as possible. Your comments will be of greater value to the student if they are stated frankly and specifically. This report will have no bearing on the student's grade. Its sole purpose is to provide the student with an objective review from a person outside of the classroom.

1. How effectively did the student initiate the interview and establish rapport with you?

2. How effective was the structure of the interview?

3. How effective were the student's questioning skills?

4. How effective were the student's communication skills: language, nonverbal communication, listening?

5. How effectively did the student close the interview?

6. What specific suggestions would you offer this student to improve his/her interviewing skills?

Interviewee's Signature _____

Interviewee's Address _____

Date of the Interview _____ Length of the Interview _____

Field Interview Critique Form

Student's Name _____ Instructor's Name _____

Please complete this form and return it as soon as possible. Your comments will be of greater value to the student if they are stated frankly and specifically. This report will have no bearing on the student's grade. Its sole purpose is to provide the student with an objective review from a person outside of the classroom.

1. How effectively did the student initiate the interview and establish rapport with you?

2. How effective was the structure of the interview?

3. How effective were the student's questioning skills?

4. How effective were the student's communication skills: language, nonverbal communication, listening?

5. How effectively did the student close the interview?

6. What specific suggestions would you offer this student to improve his/her interviewing skills?

Interviewee's Signature _____

Interviewee's Address _____

Date of the Interview _____ Length of the Interview _____